Clever Combo Quilts

Kimberly Einmo

American Quilter's Society
www.AmericanQuilter.com

Located in Paducah, Kentucky, the American Quilter's Society (AQS) is dedicated to promoting the accomplishments of today's quilters. Through its publications and events, AQS strives to honor today's quiltmakers and their work and to inspire future creativity and innovation in quiltmaking.

Senior Editor: Linda Baxter Lasco
Graphic Design: Sarah Bozone
Brady Camp
Cover Design: Sarah Bozone
Quilt Photography: Charles R. Lynch
Author's Photo: Bonnie McCaffery
Director of Publications: Kimberly Holland Tetrev

Additional copies of this book may be ordered from the American Quilter's Society, PO Box 3290, Paducah, KY 42002-3290, or online at www.AmericanQuilter.com.

Library of Congress Cataloging-in-Publication Data

Names: Einmo, Kimberly, author.
Title: Clever combo quilts / Kimberly Ein.
Description: Paducah, Kentucky : American Quilter's Society, 2016.
Identifiers: LCCN 2016050077 (print) | LCCN 2016050372 (ebook) ISBN |9781683390121 (pbk.) |ISBN 9781683395133 (ebook)
Subjects: LCSH: Patchwork--Patterns. | Quilting-- Patterns.
Classification: LCC TT835 .E4468 2016 (print) |LCC TT835 (ebook) |DDC 746.46--dc23
LC record available at https://lccn.loc.gov/2016050077

Solstice, detail. Full quilt on page 34.

In Loving Memory

Wilbur W. Wallace
November 14, 1925–November 6, 2014

Nina L. (Dale) Wallace
August 28, 1926–March 11, 2016

Dedication

I dedicate this book to my darling husband, Kent. You are the love of my life and have been my best friend for more than 28 years. I am forever grateful for your constant and unwavering support. Thank you for your love and encouragement. I also dedicate this book to the two other men in my life, our sons Joshua and Andrew. You are both amazing and gifted young men. God has blessed my life beyond measure!

Please feel free to contact me through my website or email at:

Website: www.kimberlyeinmo.com
Email: Kimberly@kimberlyeinmo.com

Contents

- **1 Pink pincushion – Confident Beginner**

The confident beginner has some rotary cutting skills, can sew an accurate ¼" seam allowance, and has experience with bias edges such as half-square and quarter square triangles.

- **2 Pink pincushions – Intermediate**

The intermediate quilter has good rotary cutting skills, sews accurate ¼" seam allowances, used different triangle units with ease and has experience working with diamonds .

- **3 Pink pincushions – Skilled Intermediate**

The skilled intermediate quilter has all the skills outlined above plus experience working with more advanced cuts and shapes such as Tri Recs units, set-in or "Y" seams, and sewing tricky intersections of multiple layers of fabrics.

Star Chain (Sangria)
54" x 54" - 1PP

Stars and Geese
64" x 64" - 1PP

Sostice
56" x 56" - 1PP

Windblown Stars
65" x 65" - 2PP

Star Flight
48" x 48" - 2PP

Spring Cabin Fever
46" x 46" - 2PP

Glacier Bay
54" x 54" - 2PP

North to Alaska
52" x 52" - 2PP

Ginger and Tea Leaves
68" x 68" - 2PP

Pinwheel Twist
54" x 54" - 3PP

The story behind the pink velvet pincushion….

Many years ago during my travels overseas, I bought a pink velvet pincushion from a tiny shop in Heidelberg, Germany. When I filmed the first (of five!) CRAFTSY classes in my home studio, the three young men on the production crew who came to film the class saw my pink pincushion and thought it was the funniest thing! They began kidding around and having fun by moving it around the set — much like an "Elf on the Shelf" — so the pink pincushion would appear in different places in different shots. This became a game and we all laughed between takes. In each of my subsequent CRAFTSY classes if you watch closely you'll see the pink pincushion in all sorts of interesting places: on top of my sewing machine, behind my head, or strategically placed on the bookshelf behind me. It seems to move like magic from one shot to the next! It became my trademark and I became known as the "quilter with the pink pincushion." Personally, I think every sassy quilter needs a pink velvet pincushion in their studio. I've added my special "magic pin" (for sewing perfect diamond points when making my signature Lone Starburst quilt) and a special ribbon with quilted blessings. If you need a pink velvet pincushion in your studio, stop by my website at: www.kimberlyeinmo.com.

Acknowledgments

They say "It takes a village," but I think it takes a posse of close friends. I'm blessed to have such wonderful friendships that have stood the test of time and circumstances. Simply put, I would not be where I am today in the quilting industry without the support and encouragement of my friends. I'd like to personally thank the following folks:

Carolyn Archer, Ohio Star Quilting. Our friendship goes back many, many years and her machine quilting has added beauty to so many of my quilts.

Miriam Fay (Carolyn Archer's Mom). I think she is personally responsible for binding 95% of the quilts in this book!

Birgit Schüller, Creative Bits. Birgit's artistic eye and machine quilting have also added so much beauty to my quilts. Yes, I really do ship my quilts overseas to Germany for her to quilt them!

Claire Neal. My dear friend with an amazing gift for precision piecing and an eye for color!

Linda Baxter Lasco. A steadfast friend and top-notch editor! Thank you for helping me with technical edits on so many levels.

I'd like to sincerely thank my publisher, Meredith Schroeder, my editor, Kimberly Tetrev, my graphic designers Sarah Bozone and Brady Camp, and all of the many creative and talented people at American Quilter's Society. I'm so grateful to have such a long-standing history with these talented and dedicated people!

A huge thank you to the following folks for their very generous support for supplying the beautiful fabrics, threads, batting, sewing machine, and furniture used to make the quilts in this book:
Hayden Lees, Timeless Treasures
Kyle Sanchez, Robert Kaufman Fabrics
Lissa Alexander, Moda Fabrics/United Notions
Bruce and Diane Madigan, SewBatik™ Fabrics
Alex Veronelli, Aurifil™ Threads
Penny McMorris, Electric Quilt® Company
Jeannie Cooke, BERNINA
John Ryan, Janome of America
Ed Moore and Susanne Voss, Koala Cabinets
Tricia Santamaria and Judy Novella, Fairfield Processing Corporation

Introduction:

Clever Combo Quilts at a Glance

Everyone loves a classic combination. Some things are just meant to go together, such as cookies and cream; chips and salsa; surf and turf; pumpkins and autumn leaves; Astaire and Rogers; cats and quilts; Facebook and friends; chocolate and, well, just about anything. (Personally, I like French fries dipped in vanilla milk shakes.) People simply love great combinations and I'm no exception. Ever since I began creating original quilt designs more than 25 years ago, I have been inexplicably drawn to putting two or more different blocks together in new and creative ways. The blocks may look lovely on their own, but look absolutely beautiful when combined. Some blocks are just meant to be set side by side and the secondary designs which emerge are both surprising and stunning!

Clever Combo Quilts is jam-packed with original quilts designed with two or more pieced block combinations. The blocks themselves are constructed from easy-to-piece units and yet the overall layout looks intricate and complicated. I guarantee these designs will look amazing no matter what colors and fabrics you choose! All you need to do is simply follow the values as listed in the recipe-style fabric requirement charts. It only takes between 5 – 7 fabrics per quilt and I'll show you how easy it is to select yardage from your stash or the quilt shop. There's no struggling to match or coordinate fabrics. The rule of thumb is this: If your fabrics look great laid out next to each other as they are listed in the chart, they will look even more spectacular when sewn into these stunning quilt designs!

Why am I so confident that your quilt will be beautiful? I've been teaching quilt classes on a national level for more than 25 years *(Golly, has it really been that long?)* and have taught hundreds of classes and thousands of students during that time. One of my well-known specialties has been designing quilts for mystery quilt classes. The students pre-select and pre-cut their fabrics to make a quilt in class and they have no idea of how it will look! These students have a great sense of adventure and fun. And my personal secret for making it work? I use shades of black, white and gray to design all my original quilt patterns using Electric Quilt software on my computer. This allows me to create the designs in grayscale, which ensures the values of lights, mediums, and darks are placed correctly within each design without the distraction of color. By following the values carefully,

LEFT AND OPPOSITE: PINWHEEL TWIST, detail. Full quilt on page 82.

any color and fabric combination will work if they are "plugged into" the right places within the design.

As for construction of the blocks I've written these patterns to be used with my own specialty ruler, the EZ® Flying Geese Ruler, which allows you to cut all your pieces and units from whole or half inch increment strips. *(No more pesky ⅞" measurements!)* You'll go beyond the basics and increase your skill level with each quilt you make. Quilters of every skill level will enjoy making these beautiful quilts! And I provide options for different color or design layout combinations and even how to create different size quilts by adding more blocks. If you're EQ software savvy, you'll definitely want to check out the add-on software for ***Clever Combo Quilts***, which features dozens of these quilt variations and a wide variety of different sizes of the quilts which are completely customizable based on your size and space requirements!

The fabric yardages for each quilt are provided as an easy shopping list and the instructions are written in a clear, recipe-style format that makes it easy to see at a glance exactly how much fabric you'll need, exactly what to cut, and how to assemble your units and blocks.

These clever combo quilts may *look* complex but only you will know how easy they actually are to construct. Be prepared to wow your friends and family with beautiful quilts made from fun and fanciful block combinations and have fun in the process. So let's get started and create your own clever combos!

Helpful Abbreviations Used In This Book

- WOF - width of fabric
- LOF - length of fabric
- HST - half-square triangle
- QST - quarter-square triangle
- RST - right sides together
- WST - wrong sides together
- RSU - right-side up

Chapter One—

Ready...

I'm so thrilled you've picked up this book and are ready to dive in to create your own beautiful quilts. I'm here as your personal quilting coach to help you throughout the entire process to ensure it will be fun and stress-free. This means I am going to make the construction process as simple as possible. Before you get started, I want to invite you to take a few minutes to *read this chapter first*. You may be so excited to begin that you're tempted skip this part, but these tips and hints will make your time spent quilting more productive and enjoyable. My goal is simply this: to help you improve your piecing skills and make beautiful quilts!

I've divided this book into easy-to-use sections designed to make the process manageable for quilters of all skill levels. Whether you are a rookie quilter or a seasoned pro, I think you'll find new ideas and clever hints designed to improve your skills. Along with the instructions in this book, I have user-friendly website I invite you to explore where you'll find lots of additional information and where you can contact me directly at www.kimberlyeinmo.com.

Some Basic Information You Should Know

This book is for quilters of all skill levels–beginners to advanced. The quilts are designed to help you improve your skills as you piece the blocks. Choose any colors or styles of fabrics you like. All you need to do is pay close attention to the values listed. Be creative with your colors and fabrics! And by all means, use your stash fabrics whenever possible. After all, most quilters are curators of their own fabric collections! The quilts in this book are designed so you can customize the sizes by simply making more blocks and adding more rows.

Pre-washing Your Fabrics - Yes or No?

This is an age old question and the answer is truly a matter of personal preference. I used to be a prewashing purist. No fabric ever entered my sewing studio that hadn't first been through the washer and dryer. But when I began making quilts using Jelly Roll bundles and precuts, prewashing wasn't at all feasible so I had to be flexible and "go with the flow." But the truth is I still prefer to prewash my fabrics and then press them with a hot iron using spray sizing to add body and a bit of stiffness back to the fabrics before I ever cut them.

Some fabrics such as saturated, dark prints and batiks, tend to have a lot of excess dye and I think it is prudent to prewash those fabrics. The time it takes to wash, dry, and press your yardage is small compared to the heartbreak of having a fabric bleed onto a light background after you have washed your finished quilt. (Ask me how I know!)

Ultimately, the choice to prewash your yardage is up to you. At the very least, test your fabrics for their colorfastness before cutting them up and sewing them into your quilts. A little prep work in advance can save you time and heartache in the end. I highly recommend those Shout® Color Catchers. They work wonders in the washing machine, both top- and front-loading washers. The old stand-by of using salt and vinegar may not work on fabrics with today's modern dyes and chemical processes. If you decide to prewash, I recommend washing your fabrics in Synthropol®, which is available at local quilt shops and from online sources.

Supplies You'll Need: Fabrics, Tools, and More Made Easy!

A place to sew – Whether you have a large, sunny studio, a small shared bedroom, or even the dining room table, the key to making your sewing are successful is to make it work for you. Arrange your space so it is organized and well-stocked with basic, quality supplies. Try to position your cutting and pressing areas within easy reach of your sewing machine. Make your space your happy place!

A good chair – A chair with proper back support is essential for pain-free time spent sewing at your machine. Perhaps consider one of those new ergonomic chairs to help alleviate back strain. It's worth the investment and your back will thank you.

Good lighting – Proper lighting is as essential, plain and simple. Natural lighting is optimum, but if you sew in the evening or if your room doesn't have access to good natural light, find the best lights you can afford and make your sewing area as bright as the surface as the sun! If possible, replace the bulbs you currently have in your lamps or overhead lighting fixtures with new, energy-efficient, full-spectrum bulbs. They will allow you to see your fabric colors more accurately and with far less eye strain. This minimal expense will yield an optimal investment in how you see your fabrics and tiny, straight stitches.

A sewing machine in good working condition – I can't emphasize it enough when I tell you that nothing in the world spoils your precious sewing time faster than a sewing machine that doesn't work properly! You'll end up feeling nothing but frustration if your machine has tension troubles or skipped stitches. Have your machine serviced regularly and clean the lint build-up *every time you change the bobbin*.

I keep a can of compressed air handy to blow out the lint from the bobbin casing area. But let me be clear: do not use the thin red nozzle

to blow air INTO the bobbin casing area. You must always bend and aim the nozzle to blow air out from back to front. Never use your mouth to blow into your machine; those moving parts do not like the moisture in your breath! A better option is one of those small hoses that attaches to your vacuum cleaner that will allow you to suck out all the lint and dust.

The important thing is to keep your sewing machine clean. Every machine deserves to go to the "spa" (an authorized dealer) for a thorough check-up at least once a year. I take my machines for a spa treatment every year when I get my mammogram. Ladies, these are two ultra-important things we need to do for our own health and the well-being of our favorite household appliance. Schedule a date on your calendar every year and stick to it!

Specialty sewing feet – You'll want to have the following presser feet to construct the quilts in this book:

- ¼" Piecing foot *(I have two; one with the guide AND one without the guide.)*
- Multi-purpose foot
- Walking foot for quilting
- Free-motion foot for quilting

Tools of the Trade

Rotary cutter –If possible, have a variety of sizes of rotary cutters on hand to accurately cut the pieces to make the quilts in this book. I prefer a 60mm but a 45mm will work just fine. You may also want to have an 18mm on hand, but I don't recommend this size for general rotary cutting. You'll find that your arm will tire easily after cutting a lot of fabric using an 18mm rotary cutter. There are many different brands of rotary cutters so do your research and "test-drive" as many as you can to find the style that fits your hand comfortably. Ask for recommendations from your friends, guild members, and local quilt shop. They may have several different cutters out of the package for you to try before you buy.

Rotary blades – When was the last time you changed your rotary blade? Don't recall? Then it's time! The rule of thumb is this: change the blade for each new project, or roughly every 8 hours of (continuous) use. However, should your blade develop a burr and begin to skip threads or cut inaccurately, or if it feels as though you're pushing it through wet sand, change the blade. You can save the used blades for cutting cardboard, wrapping paper at Christmas, or any number of other household tasks. Label the old blades properly and make sure you don't mix them up with your new ones.

Self-healing rotary cutting mat – It's amazing how many quilters I find who use a mat that is warped or deeply grooved from years of use. If the lines on your mat are chopped up from years of wear and tear, save your coupons or watch for sales and buy a new one. Remember, they put those lines on the mat for a reason! If you're in doubt about the lines on your mat because you heard an instructor or other quilting "celebrity" tell you not to use them, let me assure you the lines on the mat will allow you to measure twice and cut once! Here's how you can check for accuracy: Lay your ruler on top of the mat and line up the lines on the ruler with the lines on the mat. The lines on the mat should "disappear" underneath the lines on the ruler. I promise, it works!

Sewing machine needles – In general, you should use a size 75/10 Quilting (or Microtex or Sharp) needle for piecing. For quilting, use a size 80/11 Quilting needle or a needle matched appropriately to the type of thread you are using to machine quilt. The heavier the weight of the thread, the larger (higher size number) the needle. It is wise to keep a stash of extra needles on hand and change them frequently! The same rule of thumb applies to needles as to rotary blades: change your needle for every 8 hours of continuous use or for every new project. If you run over a pin, you might have to change the needle sooner! If you ever hear a "popping" sound as you sew, or if your machine begins to skip stitches, it is time to throw that needle away. To discard used needles, store them in empty mint or dental floss boxes.

Iron – Use an iron with plenty of steam *(Steam is our friend!)* and always keep the sole plate clean. If the sole plate is dirty or has remnants of fusible web from a previous project, buy a tube of sole plate cleaner (available at discount sewing stores, local quilt shops, and online) and clean your iron. Take care not to burn your fingers!

Ironing surface – A sturdy ironing board is essential. One that adjusts to fit your height is a blessing. If your ironing board cover is brown from years of use, invest in a clean, new cover or make your own. It's easy, inexpensive, and you can choose a pretty fabric from the remnant bin to match your room or mood!

Fabric – Use high-quality 100% cotton whenever possible. Be mindful of the thread count of fabrics from discount or bargain basement stores. Read the labels on the bolts! The lower the number of threads, the more flimsy, limp, and troublesome the fabric will be.

Thread – Use 50-wt. cotton thread in a neutral color for piecing quilts. (Avoid polyester threads if possible.) I love Aurifil 50-wt. cotton. It is thin, ultra-strong, and it produces far less lint in your machine than other brands. Plus, you can quickly and easily tell what the thread weight is by the color of the spools. (Look for the orange spools for 50-wt thread for piecing and use in your bobbin.) Remember, the lower the number of the thread weight, the thicker the thread. (12-wt. is the thickest.) 50-wt. cotton thread is ideal for piecing. The options are almost endless for the type and weight of thread you can use for quilting depending on your desired results. I tend to prefer a 28-wt. or 40-wt. for machine quilting. Do your homework and make test samples of different thread weights before actually quilting on your quilts. Thread is a quilter's ultimate eye candy. Stock up whenever you can and enjoy using a myriad of different colors!

Straight pins – I prefer the long, flat, flower head pins for pinning the seams. They are relatively inexpensive, so if your straight pins are short, rusty, or bent, throw them out and splurge on a new box. If you really want to treat yourself, buy or make a snazzy new pincushion to display all your pretty new pins. Such a mood lifter!

Batting – There are many batting options for your quilts available as well. My personal favorite types of batting are wool, bamboo, and cotton blends. Test the various types of batting and choose the type that works best for you! You'll find a list of my favorite types of batting in the Resource Guide on page 94.

Scissors – Keep shears and sharp snips for clipping threads handy at all times. I love Karen Kay Buckley's Perfect Scissors. All four sizes are available for sale on my website. I invite you to check them out.

Seam ripper – Every quilter needs one of these at some point, so make sure you use one that isn't rusty or broken as this could damage your fabrics. I can't tell you how many times my students pull out broken, dull, rusty rippers in class. A new seam ripper is such an inexpensive necessity. Treat yourself to a new one the next time you go to your local quilt shop. Then, put the cover on your old one and pitch it in the trash. You'll be so glad you did!

Specialty rulers – I'll be featuring some specialty rulers to make the quilts in this book:

EZ Flying Geese Ruler by Kimberly Einmo
EZ Jelly Roll Ruler by Kimberly Einmo
Tri-Recs Tools by Darlene Zimmerman

Acrylic rulers – At the very least you'll need a 6" x 24" acrylic ruler. However, a square ruler will be extremely helpful for squaring-up your blocks. I think the most versatile size is a 12½" square ruler. If you have other sizes of rulers, keep them handy to make the cutting easier and more efficient.

Marking tools – A mechanical pencil, Pilot FriXion pen, disappearing blue or purple ink pen, and rolling chalk markers are very helpful for making the quilts in this book. Personally, my favorite marking tool is a Hera marker. Always test these products on scraps of your fabric before marking anything on your blocks or quilt.

Basting tools – You'll likely need basting safety pins, a basting gun, or adhesive spray to help you baste your quilts. Fairfield has a wonderful new fusible batting that eliminates the need for traditional basting that is quick and easy to use with a hot iron. (Follow the manufacturer's instructions carefully.)

Fusible web – Buy it on the bolt whenever possible, and don't stock up. Yep, you read that right—don't buy fusible web too far in advance. Fusible web has a definite shelf life that can be shortened even more by exposure to heat and humidity. It can quickly become brittle or unusable. Ask me how much I've had to throw away in the past because I thought I was being thrifty buying in bulk! Generally, I prefer "lite" to the heavy-duty weight. The ultimate goal is to have quilts constructed with fusible appliqué drape beautifully!

Stabilizers – You'll need temporary or tear-away stabilizers for doing any machine appliqué. I recommend buying stabilizer on a roll instead of folded in a package. It is easier to cut just what you need from the roll and you end up wasting far less. Stock up when it goes on sale.

Basic sewing supplies – Keep a fully stocked sewing box or bin of basic sewing supplies handy at all times. It will save you hours of searching in vain for items you need close at hand. Be creative with your storage containers. Use pretty wicker baskets, nifty vinyl totes, clean berry baskets, or fabulous fabric bowls to display and keep your sewing supplies right at your fingertips!

A longarm machine quilter – If you don't plan to quilt your own quilts, take time to find someone you trust to quilt them for you. Ask for referrals at your local guild, from trusted friends, or through online forums. Schedule an appointment to meet to discuss your quilt top. It's bad manners to drop in unannounced and expect the quilter to stop in the middle of working on someone else's quilt to talk about yours. Don't be afraid to speak up and tell her or him exactly what you like and don't like. Be honest about your budget and ask for suggestions. Once you've handed off your quilt top to the longarm quilter you can move on to the next exciting quilt with a clear conscience and the longarm quilter gets a boost for business. It's a win-win situation for everyone!

Chapter Two—

Get Set…

My goal is simple: I want to make the cutting and construction process for you to be easy and accurate. So I've made the instructions for constructing the quilts to be as concise and easy to follow as possible. **This chapter is the "nuts and bolts" of everything you need to know to make the units and blocks for the quilts using my EZ Flying Geese Ruler method.**

Each project is written in a clear, recipe-style format. Simply refer to this chapter for the basic cutting and construction directions and illustrations to make the half-square triangles and flying geese units. For the Tri-Recs units, choose the ruler or templates provided. Follow the size requirements for cutting your strips and units as listed in the Cutting Instructions for each quilt. It's as simple as that!

How to Make Half-Square Triangles (HSTs) Using the EZ Flying Geese Ruler

To order the EZ Flying Geese Ruler or the EZ Jelly Roll Ruler (which is optional, but oh-so helpful!) simply go to my website at www.kimberlyeinmo.com. You may also be able to find my signature rulers at your local quilt shop or other internet sources such as Amazon.

- Place two fabric strips right sides together (RST). *NOTE: If you are right handed, begin cutting on the left side of strip unit and cut from left to right. If you are left handed, begin cutting on the right side of strip unit and cut from right to left.*
- Use Side B (the mint green side) of the ruler to cut B triangle pairs from the fabric strips, cut ½" wider than the finished size HST unit, rotating the ruler 180 degrees as shown.
- Keep the triangle pairs RST and stitch ¼" on the long side of the triangles.
- Press the seams toward the darker fabric, unless otherwise instructed.
- Trim the dog ears from the end of the HST unit.

How to Make Flying Geese Units Using the EZ Flying Geese Ruler

- Cut your fabric strips according to the ***finished*** size of flying geese units shown on the left side of Side A (magenta side) of the ruler. *NOTE: Two or four layers of fabric strips work best to avoid slippage. Six or more layers result in a loss of cutting accuracy.*
- Use Side A of the ruler to cut A (QSTs) from the fabric strips, rotating the ruler 180 degrees as shown. These are the center triangles of your flying geese units.
- To cut the side triangles for your flying geese units, fold the fabric strip in half, (RST or WST) and use Side B to cut triangles (HSTs) from the strips. This results in pairs of mirror image B triangles.
- Place a B triangle RST on top of an A triangle and stitch ¼" from the raw edge, matching the notched end to notched end and the pointed end to pointed end.
- Press the seam allowance toward the side B triangle.
- Repeat the process, sewing a B triangle to the other side of the A triangle and press the seam allowance toward the B triangle.
- Trim the dog ears on both sides. Square up the flying geese unit if necessary.

EZ Flying Geese Ruler Handy Strip Reference Chart Keep this chart nearby. It will help you calculate the number of triangles you can cut from one strip of fabric (based on a 40" strip length). Use this chart to easily convert commercial patterns to cut A and B triangles without wasting any fabric!

Strip Width	# of Triangles from Side A (QSTs)	# of Triangles from Side B (HSTs)
2"	15	26
2½"	13	24
3"	11	22
3½"	9	20
4"	8	18
4½"	7	16
5"	6	13
5½"	5	11
6"	4	9
6½"	5	10

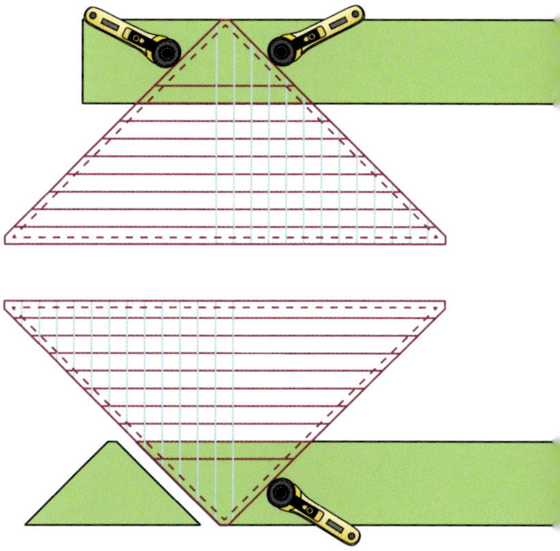
Use Side A of the EZ Flying Geese Ruler to cut A triangles (QSTs)

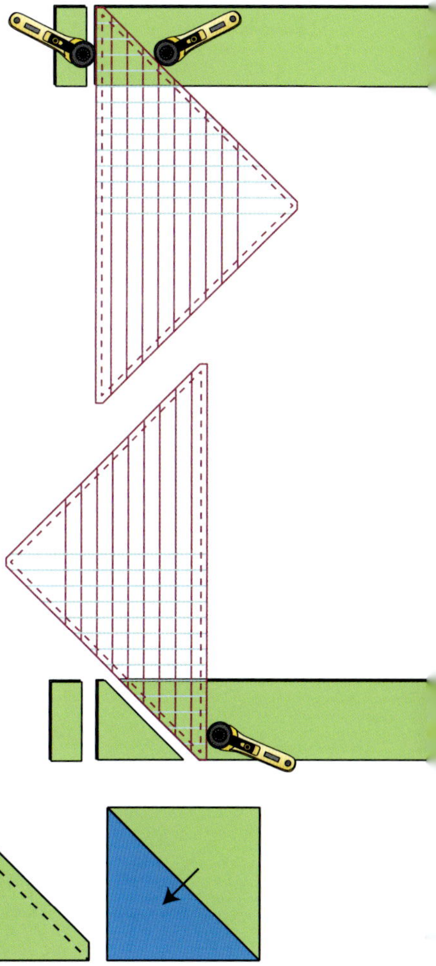
Use Side B of the EZ Flying Geese Ruler to cut B triangles (HSTs)

How to Use the EZ Jelly Roll Ruler

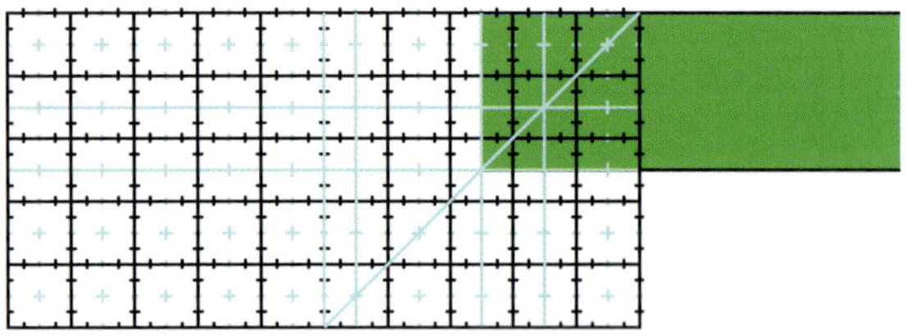

I designed this ruler to use with 2½" strips and precuts but it is my go-to ruler for cutting so many different size units! Many of the quilts in this book do not require cutting units with ⅛" increments so the EZ Jelly Roll Ruler is perfect because there are no 1/8" markings and the ruler is clear and easy to use. The size of this versatile ruler is 5" x 10" and the mint green markings show up clearly on all fabrics so you can cut your fabrics into manageable squares, rectangles, and diamonds in a snap! Of course you can use other rulers but I think once you start using this handy-dandy ruler, it will become your favorite go-to ruler as well.

How to cut squares:

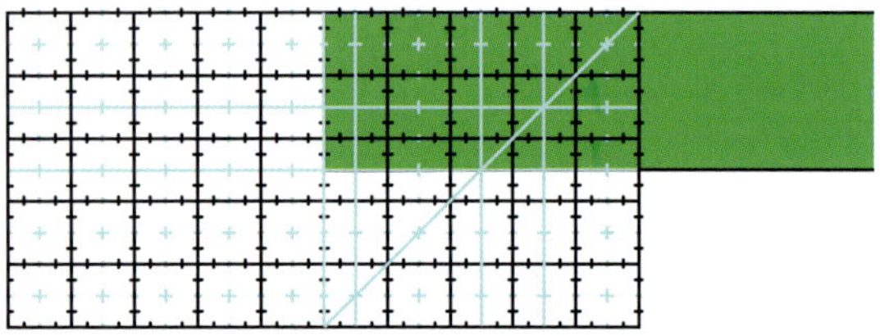

- Line up the mint green line along the edge of your strip, matching the width of your strip.
- Use the ¼", ½", or whole inch markings to cut the length of your desired unit size.
- Cut squares as shown.

How to cut rectangles:
- Line up the mint green line along the edge of your strip matching the width of your strip.
- Use the ¼", ½", or whole-inch markings to cut the length of your desired unit size.
- Cut rectangles as shown.

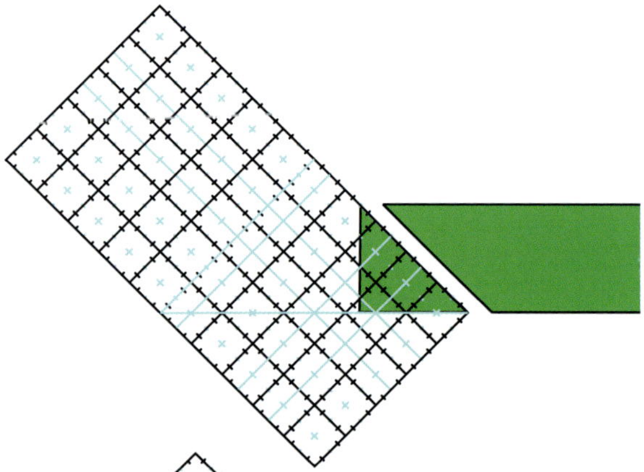

How to cut diamonds:
- Line up the 45-degree line along the bottom edge of your strip, and trim the first triangle just past the selvage.
- Slide the ruler over to the desired cutting line to match width of fabric strip to cut diamonds as shown.

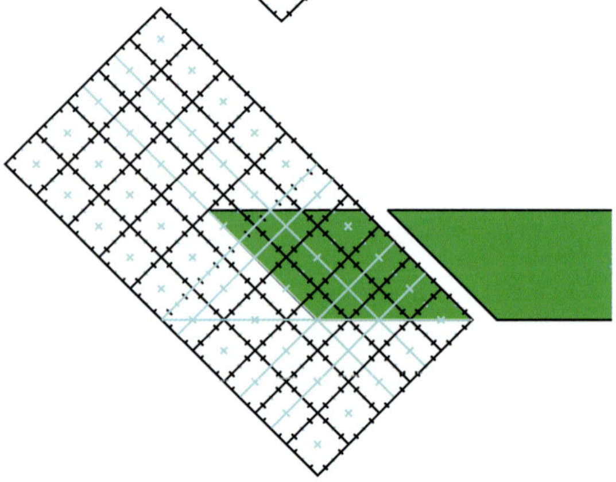

EZ Jelly Roll Ruler Handy Strip and Square Reference Table

Here are two more charts you'll definitely want to keep within easy reach. They will help you calculate the number of basic units you can cut from strips (based on a 40" strip) and precut squares. Use this chart to easily convert commercial patterns to avoid wasting fabric from your precut bundles or strips.

Size of Unit	# of Units Cut from a 5" Square	# of Units Cut from a 10" Square
1½" x 1½"	9	36
2½" x 2½"	4	16
2½" x 5"	2	8
5" x 5"	1	4
5" x 10"	0	2

Strip Width	Unit Size	# of Units Cut from a 40" Strip
1½"	1½" x 1½"	26
	1½" x 2"	20
	1½" x 2½"	16
	1½" x 3"	13
	1½" x 3½"	11
	1½" x 4"	10
	1½" x 4½"	8
	1½" x 5"	8
	1½" x 5½"	7
2½"	2½" x 2½"	16
	2½" x 3"	13
	2½" x 3½"	11
	2½" x 4"	10
	2½" x 4½"	8
	2½" x 5"	8
	2½" x 5½"	7

How to Use the TRI or RECS Tools

Use these tools to make those pesky star points for two of the quilts in this book, NORTH TO ALASKA (page 68) and PINWHEEL TWIST (page 82). Like my specialty rulers, these tools are designed to work well with strips in half- and whole-inch increments, so they are perfect to use with strips cut from the WOF.

* Cut the fabric strips as directed in the cutting instructions.
* Lay the top edge of the TRI or RECS tool along the top edge of the strip and align the bottom of the strip with the appropriate line on the tool, as directed.
* Cut on both sides of the tool.
* Rotate the tool 180 degree and align with the strip edge and continue cutting.
* With fabric units RST, lay one RECS unit on the left side of the Tri unit as shown.
* Align the angle on the RECS unit with the bottom of the TRI unit.
* Stitch ¼" from raw edge.
* Press the seam allowance toward the RECS unit.
* Repeat the process and add the other RECS unit in same manner. Press the seam allowance toward the RECS unit.
* Trim the dog ears on corners. Square up the unit if necessary.
* To piece double-rectangle units, place two RECS units RST and align the angled corners as shown.
* Stitch ¼" from the raw edge and press the seam allowance toward the darker rectangle.
* Trim the dog ears on the corners. Square up the unit if necessary.

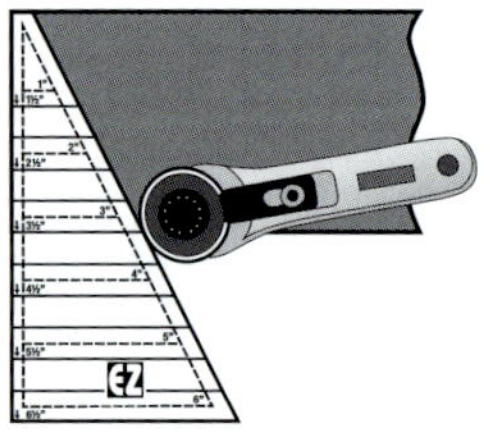

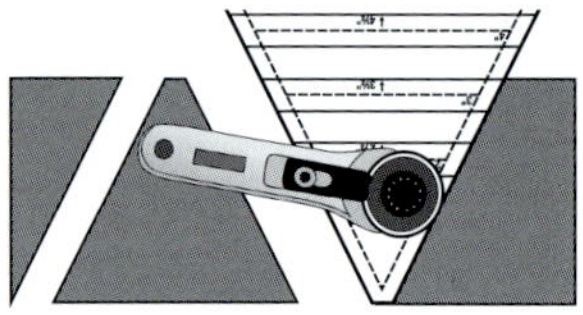

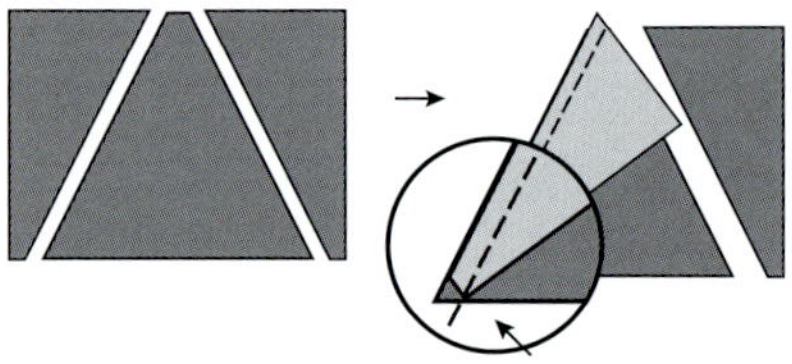

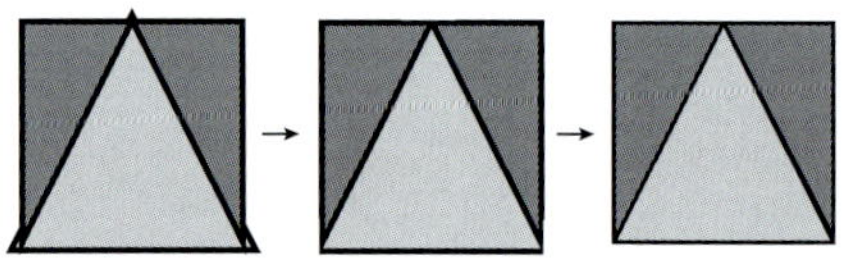

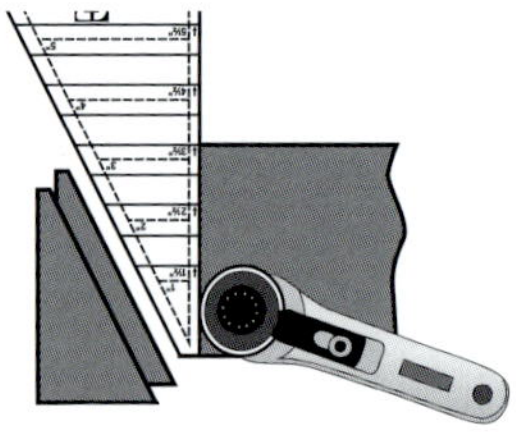

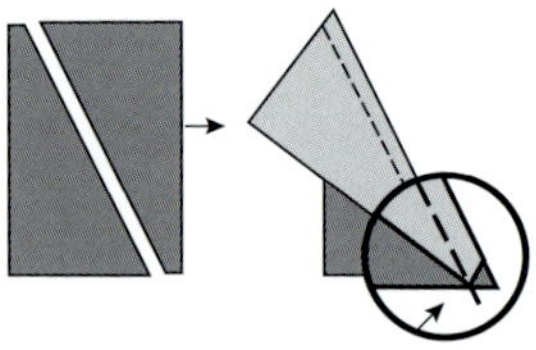

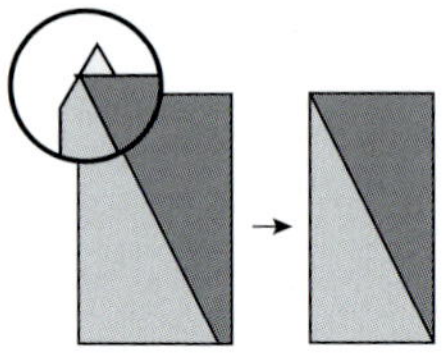

HSTs and QSTs—Here's the Difference

Have you ever wondered what the difference is between half-square triangles and quarter-square triangles? Every quilter needs to understand the basic differences. Consider a square. If you cut a square (assuming it has been cut on the straight-of-grain, as most squares should be) once diagonally, you get two triangles. The straight-of-grain runs along the two short sides of the triangle, with the bias edge running along the long side. These triangles are **half-square triangles (HSTs)** because both halves came from one square.

Consider the same square now cut twice diagonally. You get four triangles. The straight-of-grain runs along the long side of the triangle and the bias edges run along the two shorter sides. These triangles are **quarter-square triangles (QSTs)** because four triangles came from one square.

So, why is this information about the bias and the straight-of-grain important to you? Because, every quilter needs to be aware of the placement of these two types of triangles within their blocks. *The rule of thumb is this:* In most cases the straight-of-grain in every triangle needs to run along the outside edge of the completed block. Of course, there are exceptions but they are few and far between.

Now you know!

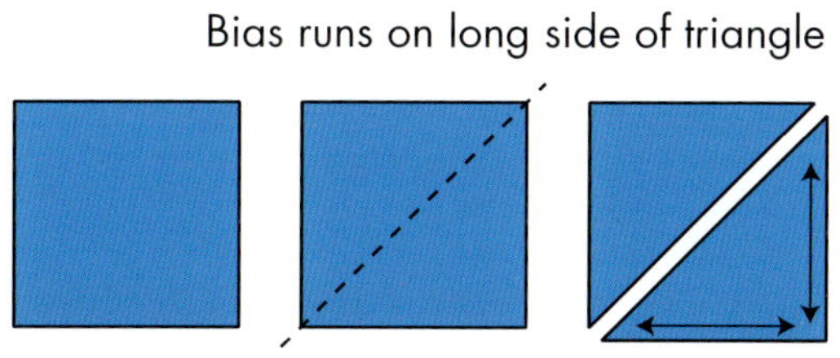

Half-square triangles:
Straight-of-grain runs along short sides of triangle

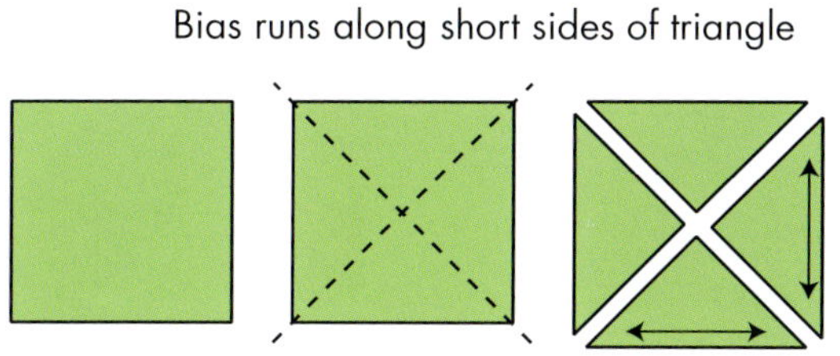

Quarter-square triangles:
Straight-of-grain runs along the long side of triangle

Clever Combo Quilts

STAR CHAIN, 54" x 54", designed by the author; made by Claire Neal; quilted by Birgit Schüller, Riegelsberg, Germany, Cretive BiTS

Star Chain

Quilt Size: 54" x 54"

Finished block size: 10" x 10"

Skill level: Skilled Beginner

This is one of my favorite patterns. It's a delightful combination of traditional-style blocks with a secondary surprise! You'll absolutely improve your precision piecing skills all the while having fun in the process. Be sure to check the quilt gallery at the end of the chapter for three more beautiful fabric/color combinations for color inspiration! (Be sure and check out my "Humble Quilt." Even pros make mistakes!)

Choose your favorite colors and fabrics according to the color ***values*** listed in the fabric requirements and arrange them from lightest to darkest. Try to avoid obviously directional or striped fabrics. The fabrics are very balanced in this quilt so if your fabrics look good lined up side-by-side, they'll look great in this quilt!

Fabric Requirements and Cutting Instructions

• Cut all strips across the WOF (selvage to selvage).

FABRIC	YARDS	INSTRUCTIONS
Fabric #1 Multi-color print *Includes outer border*	1¼ yards	• Cut (6) 5½" strips; set aside for outer border. *[Step 6]* • Cut (2) 5½" strips Subcut into (8) 5½" squares. *[Step 5]*
Fabric #2 Light Background	1¼ yards	• Cut (3) 3" strips *[Step 1]* • Cut (1) 3" strip *[Step 2]* • Cut (2) 3" strips Subcut (20) 3" squares. *[Step 3]* • Cut (2) 5½" strips Subcut (8) 5½" squares. *[Step 3]* • Cut (3) 3" strips. Use the ***EZ Flying Geese Ruler*** to cut 32 **Side A** triangles for flying geese units. *[Step 4]*
Fabric #3 Medium/Light	⅓ yard	• Cut (3) 3" strips Subcut (32) 3" squares. *[Steps 3 and 5]*

(continued)

(continued)

FABRIC	YARDS	INSTRUCTIONS
Fabric #4 Medium	½ yard	• Cut (1) 3" strip. *[Step 2]* • Cut (4) 3" strips; fold strips RST and use the ***EZ Flying Geese Ruler*** to cut 32 PAIRS of **Side B** triangles. *[Step 4]*
Fabric #5 Dark	⅓ yard	• Cut (3) 3" strips. *[Step 1]*
Fabric #6 Inner Border	½ yard	• Cut (4) 3" strips for inner border *[Step 6]*
Backing	3½ yards	• 2 panels 30" x 60"
Batting		• 60" x 60"
Binding	½ yard	• Cut (6) – 2¼" strips. Join end-to-end.

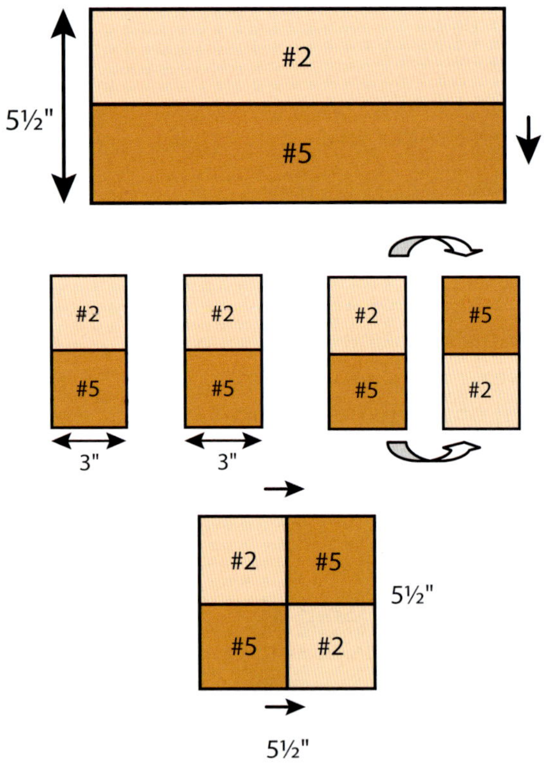

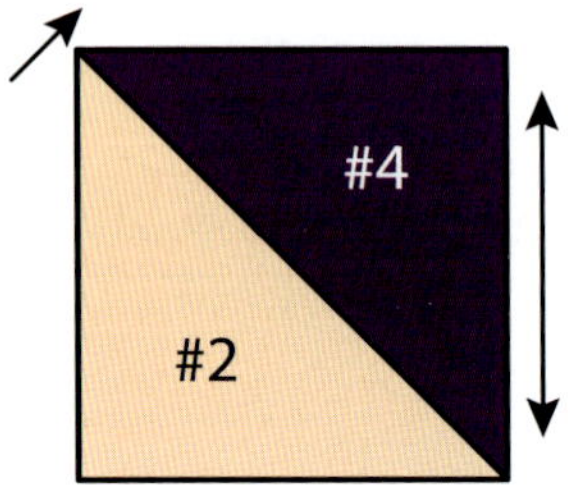

3" unfinished

Step 1: Construct the Four-Patch Units

- Sew 3" strips of fabrics #2 and #5 into a strip-set as shown. Press the seams toward the darker fabric. Repeat to make a total of 3 strip-sets.
- Cut 32 – 3" segments.
- Sew 2 segments together, rotating one segment as shown, to make a four-patch unit. Press the seam open. Make 16.
- The four-patch units should measure 5½" x 5½" unfinished. Square up if necessary.

TOP TIP!

I like to use the Strip Stick; it really helps to press the seams open and make the units lie flat!

Step 2: Construct the HSTs

- Place the fabric #2 and fabric #4 – 3" strips RST.
- Use **Side B** of the ***EZ Flying Geese Ruler*** to cut 16 – 3" triangle PAIRS. Refer to page 16 for directions to cut, sew, and trim the triangle units to make 16 HSTs. Press the seam allowance toward the darker fabric.
- The HSTs should measure 3" x 3" unfinished. Square up if necessary.

Step 3: Construct the Chain Block

Use the following units to construct each block:

- (1) fabric #1 – 3" square
- (1) fabric #2 – 5½" square
- (1) fabric #3 – 3" square
- (2) four-patch units
- (2) HSTs

Make (8) blocks.

The blocks should measure 10½" square unfinished.

Square up if necessary.

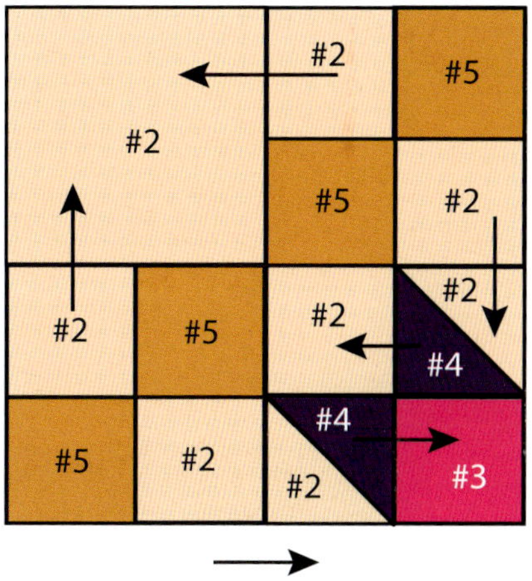

Step 4: Construct the Flying Geese Units

Refer to pages 16 and 17 for directions to make 32 flying geese units using:

- 64 fabric #4 B triangles
- 32 fabric #2 A triangles
- Press the seams away from the center triangle.
- The flying geese units should measure 3" x 6" unfinished. Square up if necessary.

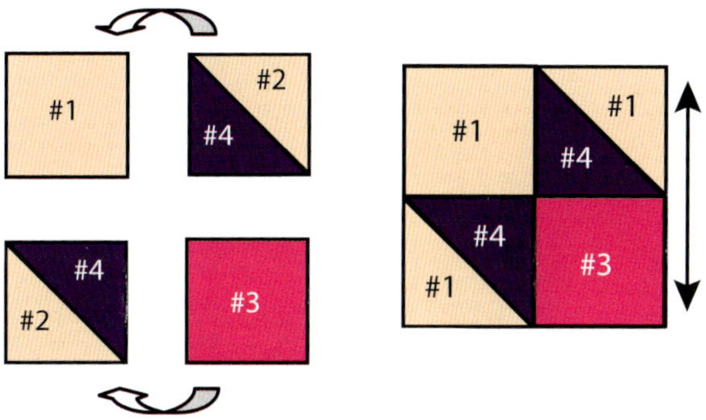

Step 5: Construct the Star Blocks

Use the following units to create each block:

- 2 fabric #2 and 2 fabric #3 – 3" squares for the Version A blocks and one fabric #2 and three fabric #3 – 3" squares for the Version B blocks
- One fabric #1 – 5½" square
- 4 flying geese units

- Make 4 each.
- The blocks should measure 10½" x 10½" unfinished. Square up if necessary.

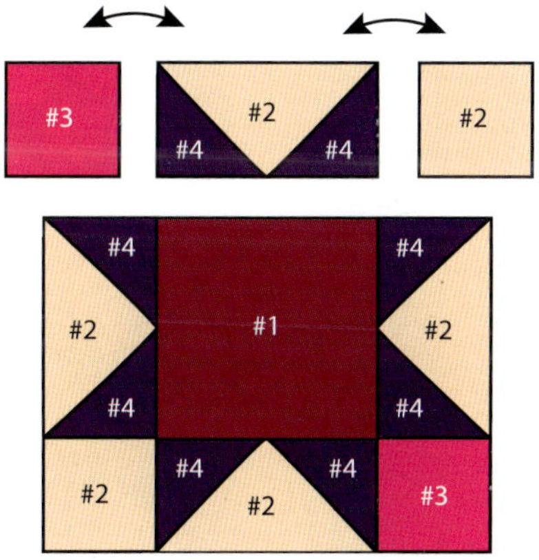

Version A - Make 4.

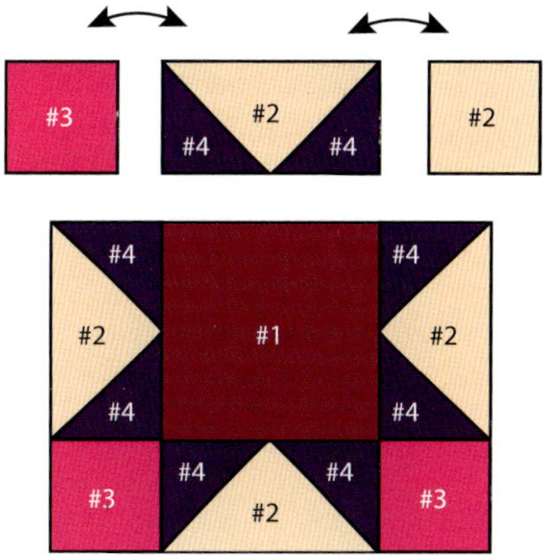

Version B - Make 4.

Step 6: Construct the Quilt Top

- Layout the blocks as shown in the diagram, rotating the blocks as needed.
- Sew the blocks into rows; sew the rows together.
- Add the 3" fabric #6 inner borders with the fabric #3 squares in the corners. Press the seams away from the quilt center.
- Add the 5½" fabric #1 outer border. Press the seams away from the quilt center.

Quilt assembly

Flip Flops

Designed and made by the author; quilted by Carolyn Archer, Ohio Star Quilting

I used this Star Chain pattern to teach as a mystery quilt class on a cruise to the Mexican Riviera. The tropical, flip flop batik fabric instantly caught my eye! I adore batik fabrics so it was easy to choose complementary colors that give this quilt the feel of pristine, sandy beaches with my toes in the sand.

Rhapsody

Designed and made by the author; quilted by Carolyn Archer, Ohio Star Quilting

These elegant print fabrics were so rich and luxurious, I just knew they would look amazing sewn into this design! I love saturated, jewel-tones and the pattern constructed using these pretty paisleys hits all the right notes!

Humble Quilt

Designed and made by the author and quilted by Carolyn Archer, Ohio Star Quilting

I made this quilt top and sent it to my dear friend Carolyn, who quilted it beautifully. It wasn't until I got the quilt back and hung it on my wall I noticed the error: one of the blocks was turned and pieced into the top incorrectly! This is a case of two quilt "professionals" who didn't see the mistake throughout the entire construction process because we were both focused so intently and I didn't step back to see the entire design. Hence, it is my humble quilt because it reminds me that only God makes perfect things.

Stars and Geese, 64" x 64", designed by the author; made by Claire Neal, Hampton Roads, VA; and quilted by Carolyn Archer, Ohio Star Quilting

Stars and Geese

Quilt size: 64" x 64"

Finished block size: 10" x 10"

Skill level: Skilled Beginner

I admit it; I'm a total pushover for star blocks! Sawtooth Stars are my particular favorite because they are constructed using simple squares and my all-time favorite unit in quilting—flying geese! Why, you ask? Because they are so completely versatile! Almost no other pieced unit used in quilting provides such a wide range of options for blocks. The combinations with other simple, pieced units are indeed endless! Best of all, flying geese units can be made using a basic, traditional method or with my signature method using the EZ Flying Geese Ruler. You can make them using no math, no wasted fabric, and of most important of all, no stress! Your quilt will be stunning and I've provided two sizes from which to choose!

Fabric Requirements and Cutting Instructions

• Cut all strips across the WOF (selvage to selvage).

Large Quilt 64" x 64"

FABRIC	YARDAGE	CUTTING INSTRUCTIONS
Fabric #1 Multicolor print *Outer border*	1¼ yards	• Cut (7) 5½" strips; set aside for the outer border.
Fabric #2 Light *Background*	1½ yards	• Cut (4) 3" strips; subcut (52) 3" squares. *[Step 3]* • Cut (2) 10½" strips; subcut (24) 3" x 10½" rectangles. *[Step 2]* • Cut (5) 3" strips; use the ***EZ Flying Geese Ruler*** to cut (52) **Side A** triangles. *[Step 1]*
Fabric #3 Dark *Stars*	1¼ yards	• Cut (2) 5½" strips; subcut (14) 5½" squares. *[Step 3]* • Cut (10) 3" strips; fold strips RST and use ***EZ Flying Geese Ruler*** to cut 100 PAIRS of **Side B** triangles. *[Step 1]*
Fabric #4 Medium	¼ yard	• Cut (2) 3" strips; use the ***EZ Flying Geese Ruler*** to cut (12) **Side A** triangles. *[Step 1]*
Fabric #5 Medium	¼ yard	• Cut (2) 3" strips; use the ***EZ Flying Geese Ruler*** to cut (12) **Side A** triangles. *[Step 1]*

(continued)

(continued)

FABRIC	YARDAGE	CUTTING INSTRUCTIONS
Fabric #6 Medium	¼ yard	• Cut (2) 3" strips; use the ***EZ Flying Geese Ruler*** to cut (12) **Side A** triangles. *[Step 1]*
Fabric #7 Medium *Includes inner border*	¾ yard	• Cut (6) 2½" strips; piece together for the inner border. • Cut (2) 3" strips; use the ***EZ Flying Geese Ruler*** to cut (12) **Side A** triangles. *[Step 1]*
Backing	4¼ yards	• 2 panels 36" x 72"
Batting	–	• 72" x 72"
Binding	½ yard	• Cut (8) 2¼" strips. Join end-to-end.

Small Quilt 44" x 44"

FABRIC	YARDAGE	CUTTING INSTRUCTIONS
Fabric #1 Multi-color print *Outer border*	1¼ yards	• Cut strips for fabric #1 ONLY along the LOF. • Cut (4) 5½" strips; set aside for the outer border.
Fabric #2 Light *Background*	1 yard	• Cut (7) 3" strips; subcut (20) 3" squares *[Step 3]* and (8) 3" x 10½" rectangles. *[Step 2]* • Cut (2) 3" strips; use the ***EZ Flying Geese Ruler*** to cut 20 **Side A** triangles. *[Step 1]*
Fabric #3 Dark *Stars*	¾ yard	• Cut (1) 5½" strip; subcut (5) 5½" squares. *[Step 3]* • Cut (4) 3" strips; fold strips RST and use ***EZ Flying Geese Ruler*** to cut 36 PAIRS of **Side B** triangles. *[Step 1]*
Fabric #4 Medium	¼ yard	• Cut (1) 3" strip; use the ***EZ Flying Geese Ruler*** to cut 4 **Side A** triangles. *[Step 1]*
Fabric #5 Medium	¼ yard	• Cut (1) 3" strip; use the ***EZ Flying Geese Ruler*** to cut 4 **Side A** triangles. *[Step 1]*
Fabric #6 Medium	¼ yard	• Cut (1) 3" strip; use the ***EZ Flying Geese Ruler*** to cut 4 **Side A** triangles. *[Step 1]*

(continued)

(continued)

FABRIC	YARDAGE	CUTTING INSTRUCTIONS
Fabric #7 Medium *Includes inner border*	¾ yard	• Cut (6) 2½" strips; piece together for inner border. • Cut (1) 3" strip; use the ***EZ Flying Geese Ruler*** to cut 4 **Side A** triangles. *[Step 1]*
Backing	3 yards 2¾ yards	• 2 panels 25" x 50"
Batting	–	• 50" x 50"
Binding	½ yard	• Cut (5) 2¼" strips. Join end-to-end.

NOTE: In each step, the amounts needed for the large quilt are given, followed by the amounts needed for the small quilt, given in parentheses.

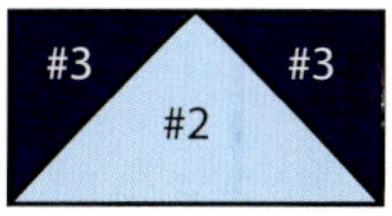

Make 52 (for the large quilt).
Make 20 (for the small quilt).

Step 1: Construct the Flying Geese Units

Refer to pages 16 and 17 for directions to make 52 (20) flying geese units using:

- 104 (40) fabric #3 B triangles
- 52 (20) fabric #2 A triangles
- Make 12 (4) flying geese units using:
    - 24 (8) fabric #3 B triangles
    - 12 (4) fabric #4 A triangles
- Make 12 (4) flying geese units using:
    - 24 (8) fabric #3 B triangles
    - 12 (4) fabric #5 A triangles
- Make 12 (4) flying geese units using:
    - 24 (8) fabric #3 B triangles
    - 12 (4) fabric #6 A triangles
- Make 12 (4) flying geese units using:
    - 24 (8) fabric #3 B triangles
    - 12 (4) fabric #7 A triangles
- Press the seams toward the side triangles. The units should measure 3" x 6" unfinished. Square up if necessary.

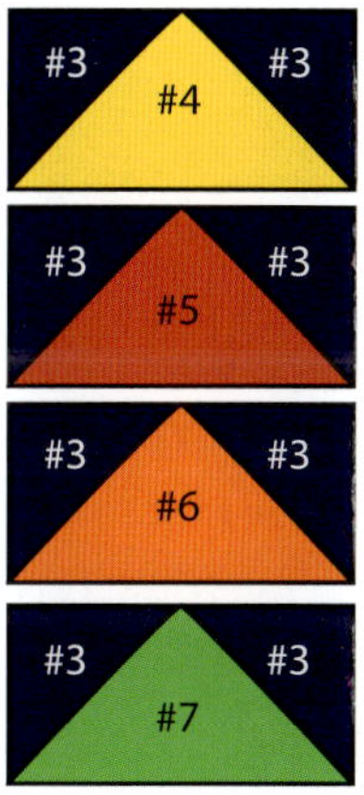

Make 12 of each color (for the large quilt).
Make 4 of each color (for the small quilt).

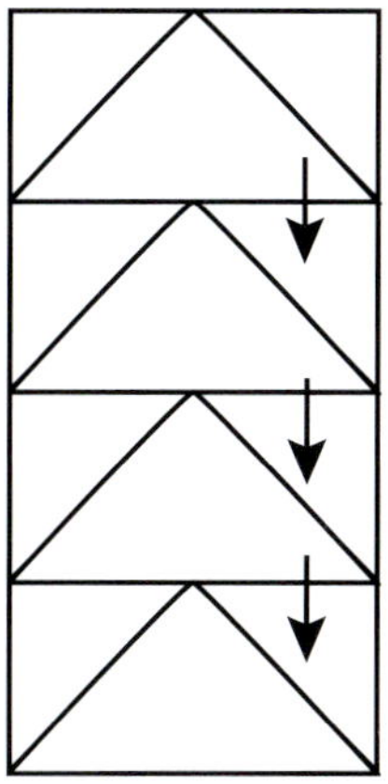

Step 2: Construct the Flying Geese Blocks

- Sew the flying geese units together in the order shown.
- Press the seams in the direction of the arrows.
- Sew two fabric #2 – 3" x 10½" rectangles on either side of the flying geese units.
- Press the seams toward the rectangles.
- The blocks should measure 10½" x 10½" unfinished. Square up if necessary.

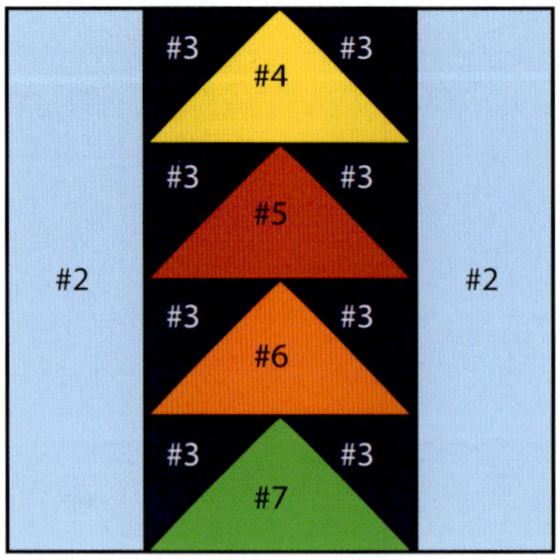

Step 3: Construct the Sawtooth Star Blocks

- Add fabric #3 – 3" squares on both sides of half of the flying geese units. Press the seams toward squares.
- Sew the remaining flying geese units to both sides of fabric #2 – 5½" squares. Press the seams toward the squares.
- Assemble blocks in rows; sew the rows together.
- The blocks should measure 10½" x 10½". unfinished. Square up if necessary.

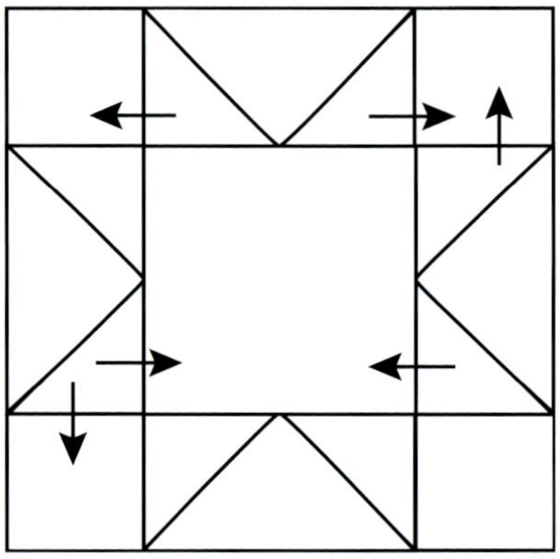

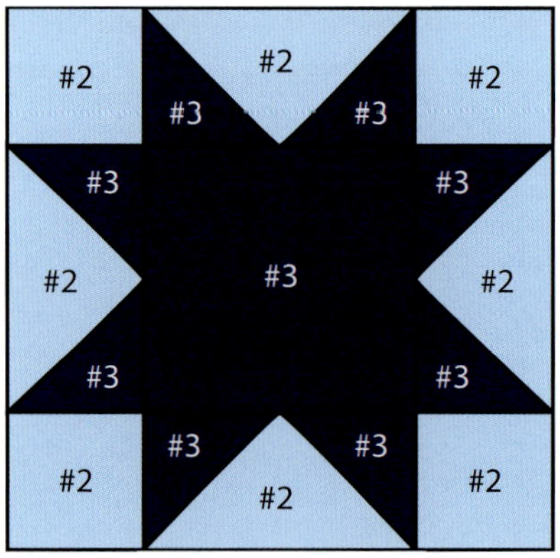

Step 4: Construct the Quilt Top

- Lay out the blocks in rows, following the diagram for your chosen size. Join the rows; sew the rows together.
- Add the inner borders. Press the seams away from the quilt center.
- Add outer borders and press the seams away from the quilt center.

Quilt assembly

Swirls

Designed and made by the author and quilted by Carolyn Archer, Ohio Star Quilting

True confession: I wanted to use up some fabric in my stash and I was drawn to the bold, modern print in the border. When I finished making the quilt, I eagerly took it to my local quilting group for show and tell. When one of my friends saw the quilt she loudly exclaimed, "It looks like there are nipples all over the border!" So from that time on, this has been cheekily called The Nipple Quilt. Now you know the real story! It measures 44" x 44".

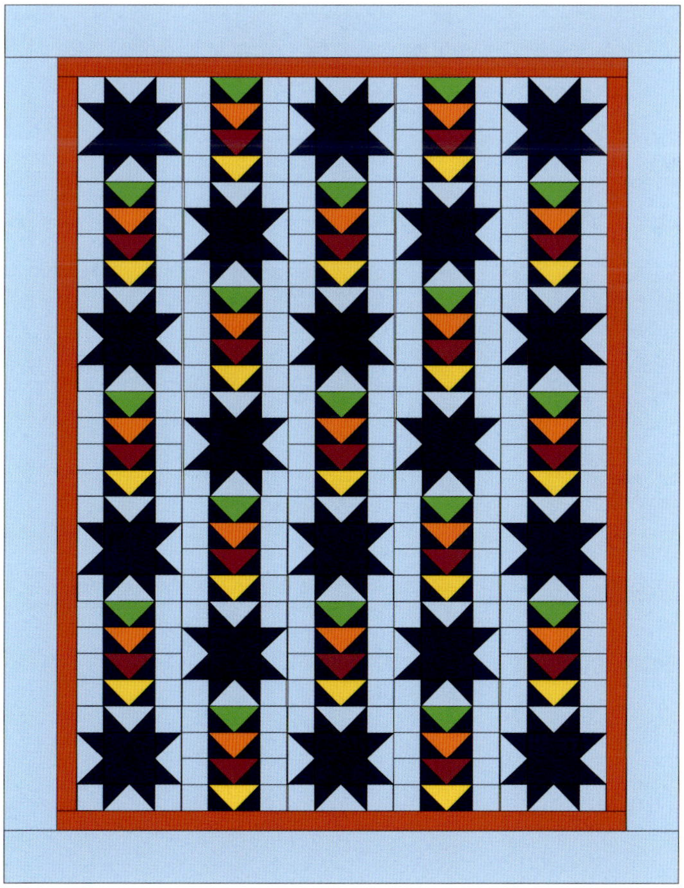

Bonus Layout!

Would you like to make this quilt into a rectangular shape to fit a twin size bed, rather than a square quilt? Or, would you like a more modern, less traditional feel to this design? Try this layout. You'll need 18 Sawtooth Star blocks and 17 Flying Geese blocks. It measures 64" x 84".

SOLSTICE, 56" x 56", designed and made by the author; quilted by Carolyn Archer, Ohio Star Quilting

SOLSTICE

Quilt size: 56" x 56"

Finished block size: 14" x 14"

Skill level: Skilled Beginner

This is combo quilting at its best! Two similar, yet delightfully different, star blocks, surrounded by easy-to-piece double-rectangle units, create a secondary design that is truly eye-catching! All you need to do is select fabrics that make you happy, beginning with a multi-color, focus print fabric. Choose one you love—a fabric that makes your heart sing! Then select a background fabric such as a solid, tone-on-tone, or something that "reads" like a solid. Next, select coordinating colors found in your multi-color print that have a lot of contrast with each other and the background. Simply follow the values listed on the fabric supply list carefully and they will look dynamite in this stunning design!

Fabric Requirements and Cutting Instructions

• Cut all strips across the WOF (selvage to selvage).

FABRIC	YARDS	INSTRUCTIONS
Fabric #1 Light background	3 yards	• Cut (12) 1½" strips. *[Step 2]* • Cut (4) 3" strips. Use the ***EZ Flying Geese Ruler*** to cut 36 **Side A** triangles. *[Step 3]* • Cut (3) 3" strips; subcut (36) 3" x 3" squares. *[Step 4]* • Cut (5) 2½" strips; cut (72) 2½" x 2½" squares. *[Steps 2 & 5, 36 each]* • Cut (3) 6½" strips; subcut (48) 2½" x 6½" rectangles for the sashing. *[Step 6]* • Cut (7) 3½" strips for the border. *[Step 6]*
Fabric #2 Multicolor print	⅜ yards	• Cut (2) 3" strips. Use the ***EZ Flying Geese Ruler*** to cut 20 PAIRS of **Side B** triangles *[Step 3]* • Cut (1) 5½" strip; cut (5) 5½" x 5½" squares. *[Step 4]*
Fabric #3 Medium	¼ yard	• Cut (1) 3" strip. *[Step 1]* • Cut (1) 3" strip; fold in half and use the ***EZ Flying Geese Ruler*** to cut 8 PAIRS of Side B triangles. *[Step 3]*
Fabric #4 Medium	¼ yard	• Cut (1) 3" strip. *[Step 1]* • Cut (1) 3" strip; fold in half and use the ***EZ Flying Geese Ruler*** to cut 8 PAIRS of **Side B** triangles. *[Step 3]*.

(continued)

(continued)

FABRIC	YARDS	INSTRUCTIONS
Fabric #5 Dark	⅜ yard	• Cut (6) 1½" strips. *[Step 2]*
Fabric #6 Medium dark	⅜ yard	• Cut (7) 1½" strips. *[Step 2]*
Fabric #7 Medium	⅛ yard	• Cut (1) 2½" strip; subcut (16) 2½" x 2½" squares for the cornerstones. *[Step 7]*
Backing	3½ yards	• 2 panels 30" x 60"and piece for the backing
Batting		• 60" x 60"
Binding	½ yard	• Cut (6) – 2½" strips. Join end-to-end.

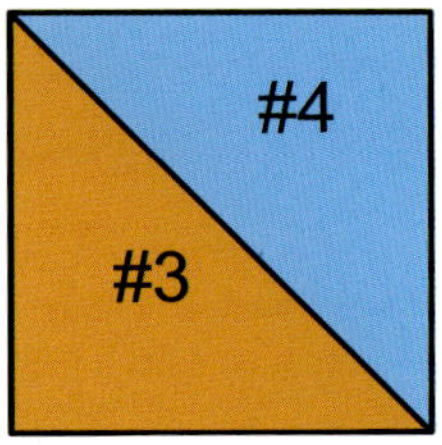

Make 16 - 3" x 3" unfinished.

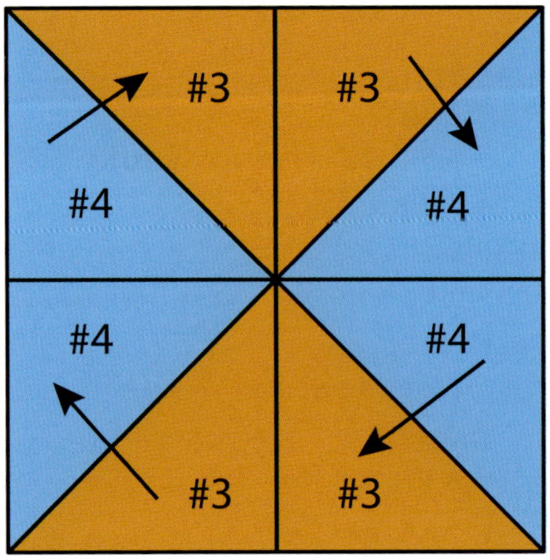

Make 4 - 5½" x 5½" unfinished.

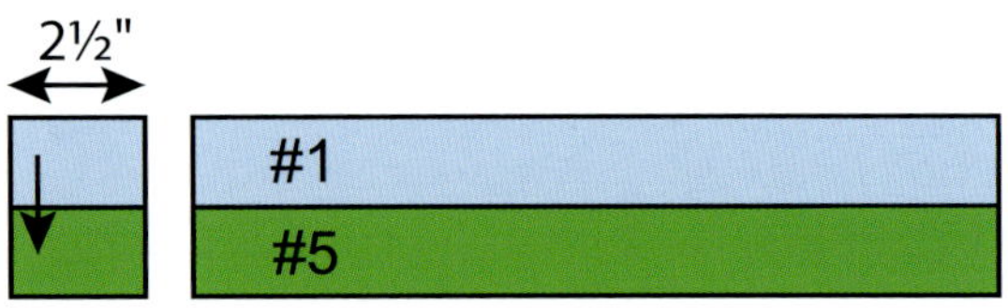

Cut 68. *Make 5.*

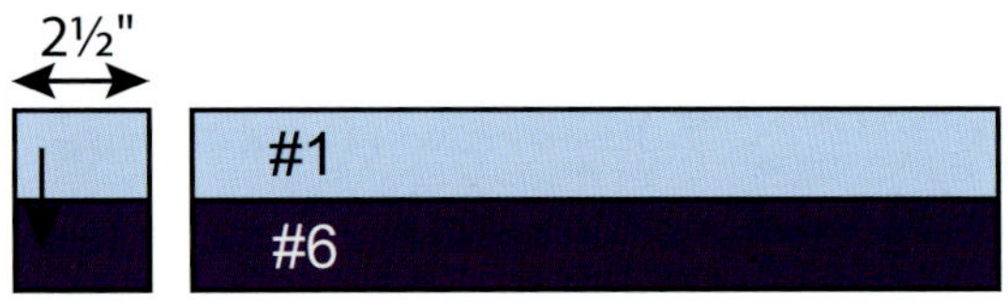

Cut 88. *Make 6.*

Step 1: Construct the HSTs

- Place the fabric #3 and fabric #4 – 3" strips RST.
- Use **Side B** of the **EZ Flying Geese Ruler** to cut 16 – 3" triangle PAIRS. Refer to page 16 for directions to cut, sew , and trim the triangle units to make 16 HSTs.
- Press the triangle units closed to set the seams; **then press seam allowances of 8 of the units toward fabric #3 and 8 of the units toward fabric #4.**
- The HSTs should measure 3" x 3" unfinished. Square up if necessary.
- Lay out the HSTs as shown and sew into four-patch units, noting the position of the differently pressed seam allowances. Be careful to follow the orientation of the HSTs exactly!
- Press the last seam open so the block lies flat.
- Make 4 four-patch units.
- The four-patch units should measure 5½" x 5½" unfinished. Square up if necessary.

Step 2: Construct the Double-Rectangle Units

- Sew 1½" strips of fabrics #1 and #5 into a strip-set as shown. Press the seams toward fabric #5. Repeat to make a total of 5 strip-sets.
- Subcut 68 – 2½" #1/#5 double-rectangle units.
- Sew 1½" strips of fabrics #1 and #6 into strip-sets as shown. Press the seams toward fabric #6.

- Repeat to make a total of 6 #1/#6 strip-sets.
- Subcut 88 – 2½" #1/#6 double-rectangle units.
- Sew 1½" strips of fabrics #5 and #6 into one strip-set as shown. Press the seam toward fabric #6.
- Subcut 12 – 2½" #5/#6 double-rectangle units.
- Use 20 fabric #1 – 2½" x 2½" squares and 80 #1/#5 double-rectangle segments to create 5 double-rectangle units as shown.
- Press the seams toward the fabric #1 squares.
- Use 16 fabric #1 – 2½" x 2½" squares and 64 #1/#6 double-rectangle segments to create 4 double-rectangle units as shown.
- Press the seams toward the fabric #1 squares.
- Set aside the remaining 8 – #1/#6, 4 – #1/#5, and 12 – #5/#6 double-rectangle units for Step 5.

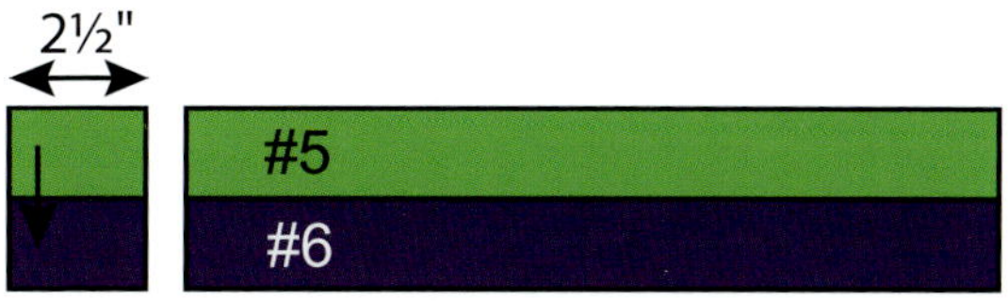

Cut 12. Make 1.

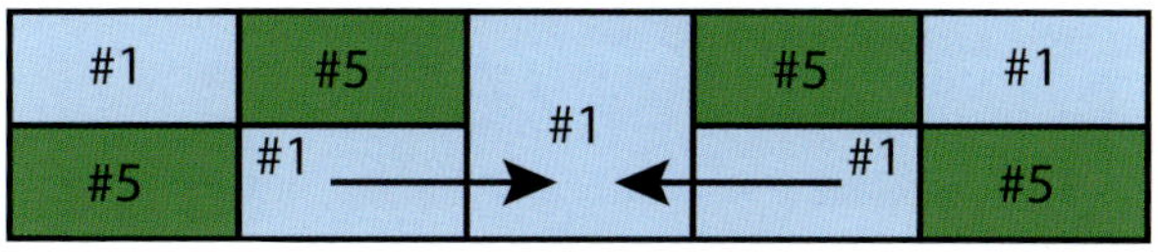

Make 20.

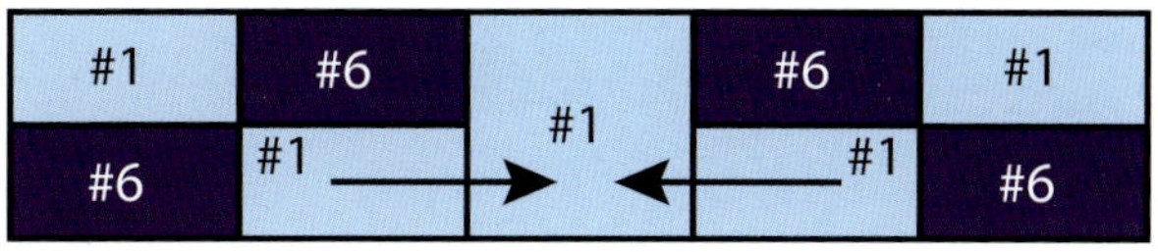

Make 16.

Step 3: Construct the Flying Geese Units

- Refer to pages 16 & 17 for directions to make 36 flying geese units.
- Make 8 using 8 fabric #1 A triangles and 8 PAIRS #3 B triangles.
- Make 8 using 8 fabric #1 A triangles and 8 PAIRS #4 B triangles.
- Make 20 using 20 fabric #1 A triangles and 20 PAIRS fabric #2 B triangles.
- Press the seams away from the center triangle.
- The flying geese units should measure 3" x 6" unfinished. Square up if necessary.
- Trim all dog ears, and square up if necessary.
- The units should measure 3" x 6". Square up if necessary.

#1/#3 - Make 8.

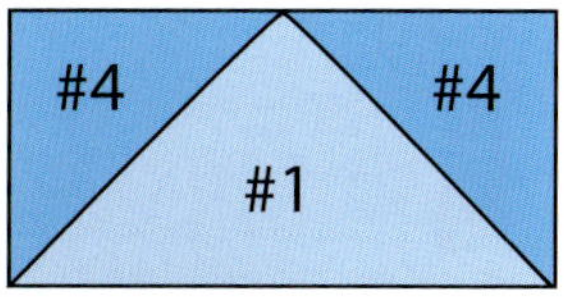

#1/#4 - Make 8.

#1/#2 - Make 20.

Step 4: Star Block Assembly

- Use the following units to construct each Sawtooth Star block as shown:
  - 1 fabric #2 – 5½" x 5½" square for the center
  - 4 – #1/#2 flying geese units
  - 4 fabric #1 – 3" x 3" squares at the corners
- Make 5 blocks. The blocks should measure 10½" x 10½" unfinished. Square up if necessary.
- Use the following units to construct each Chevron Star block as shown:
  - One 5½" x 5½" four-patch unit for the center.

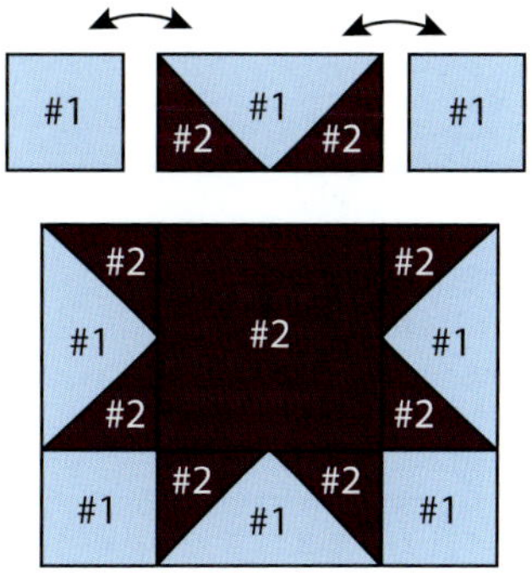

Make 5.

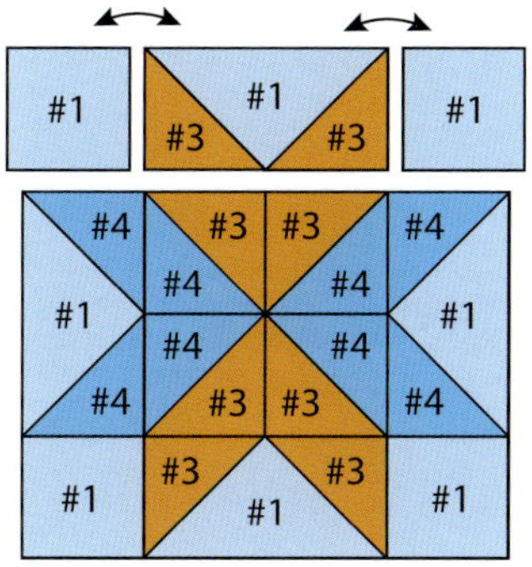

Make 4.

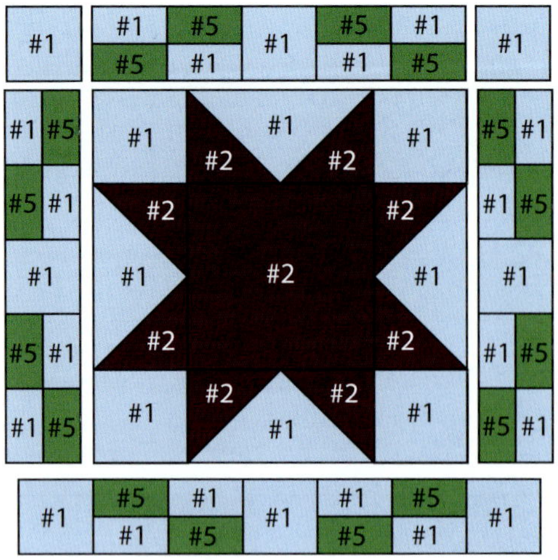

Make 5.

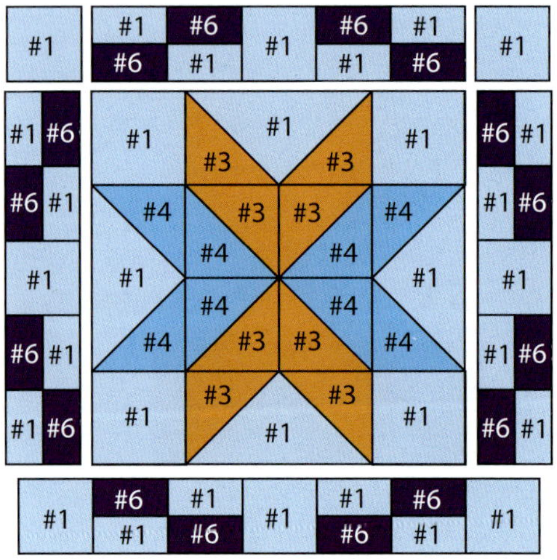

Make 4.

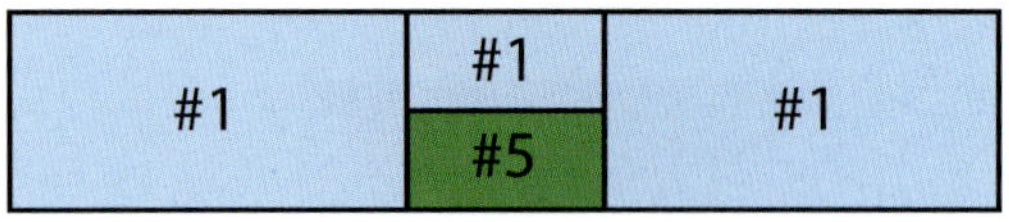

Make 8 with #1/#6 units.

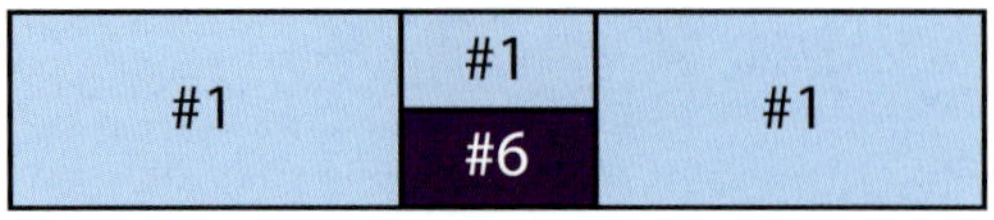

Make 4 with #1/#5 units.

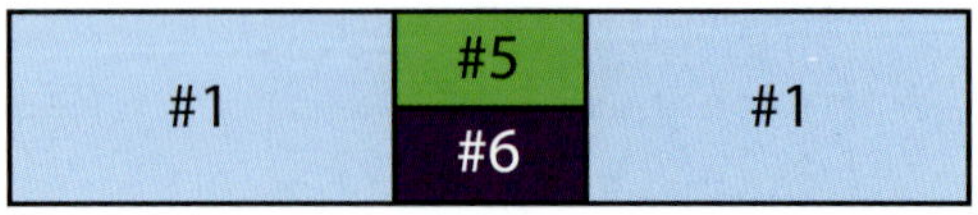

Make 12 with #5/#6 units.

- 2 – #1/#3 flying geese units
- 2 – #1/#4 flying geese units
- 4 fabric #1 – 3" x 3" squares at the corners.

- Make 4 blocks. The blocks should measure 10½" x 10½" unfinished. Square up if necessary.

Step 5: Star Block Frame Assembly

- Each of the Star blocks will be "framed" as shown using the rectangle units constructed in Step 3.
- For each Sawtooth Star block, use:
  - 4 fabric #1 – 2½" x 2½" squares
  - 4 – #1/#6 rectangle units
  - Make 5.
- For each Chevron Star block, use:
  - 4 fabric #1 – 2½" x 2½" squares
  - 4 –#1/#5 rectangle units
  - Make 4.
- Add the appropriate rectangle units to the sides of each block.
- Join 2 fabric #1 squares to the ends of each of the remaining rectangle units.
- Add to the top and bottom of the each block.
- The blocks should measure 14½" x 14½" unfinished.
- Square up if necessary.

Step 6: Sashing Assembly

- Construct the pieced sashing units as shown:
  - Make 8 using 16 fabric #1 – 2½" x 6½" rectangles and 8 fabrics #1/#6 double-rectangle units.
  - Make 4 using 8 fabric #1 – 2½" x 6½" rectangles and 4 fabrics #1/#5 double-rectangle units.
  - Make 12 using 24 fabric #1 – 2½" x 6½" rectangles and 8 fabrics #5/#6 double-rectangle units.
- Press the seams away from the double-rectangle units.
- The pieced sashing strips should measure 2½" x 14½".

Step 7: Quilt Top Assembly

- Arrange the pieced sashing strips and cornerstones as shown. Position the 5 Sawtooth Star blocks at the four corners and in the center and the Chevron Star blocks in the remaining spaces.
- Sew the components into rows; sew the rows together. Press.
- Add fabric #1 – 3½" border strips to the sides first, then to the top and bottom of the quilt.

Quilt assembly

Bonus Layouts

You can really get creative with this design by changing the placement of the fabrics in the sashing! This design is easily adaptable to a wide variety of sizes simply by adding more blocks. If you'd like to experiment, copy the following layout options on your printer and cut out the blocks with scissors. You can try positioning the blocks in any number of arrangements for a truly personal and unique layout. Most of all, have fun!

Windblown Stars, 66" x 66", designed and made by the author; quilted by Carolyn Archer, Ohio Star Quilting

Windblown Stars

Quilt size: 65" x 65"

Finished block size: 10" x 10"

Skill level: Confident Beginner

This pretty design celebrates the blustery winds of spring on a starry evening! Constructed using just two blocks, this particular two-block combo happens to be one of my personal favorites—simple yet eye-catching. This would also look beautiful in a planned-scrappy version. Simply use those fabrics you have in your stash and group them together by colors to make this design work. You'll have this whipped up in absolutely no time at all, and by adding more blocks, you'll be able to customize the size with no problem!

Fabric Requirements and Cutting Instructions

• Cut all strips across the WOF (selvage to selvage).

FABRIC	YARDS	INSTRUCTIONS
Fabric #1 Multi-color print	1¼ yards	• Cut (6) 6" strips for the outer borders. (Optional: See Step 5.)
Fabric #2 Light background	1¼ yards	• Cut (10) 3" strips; subcut 100 **Side A** triangles. *[Step 1]* • Cut (5) 3" strips; subcut 96 (48 PAIRS) of **Side B** triangles. *[Step 3]*
Fabric #3 Medium light	1 yard	• Cut (5) 3" strips; subcut 104 (52 pairs) of **Side B** triangles. *[Step 3]* • Cut (2) 5½" strips; subcut (13) 5½" x 5½" squares. *[Step 2]*
Fabric #4 Medium	¾ yard	• Cut (5) 3" strips; subcut 48 **Side A** triangles. *[Step 3]*
Fabric #5 Medium dark	½ yard	• Cut (3) 3" strips; subcut 48 **Side B** triangles (NOT pairs!) ***from fabric strips facing WRONG SIDE UP***. *[Step 3]*
Fabric #6 Dark	¾ yard	• Cut (3) 3" strips; subcut 48 **Side B** triangles (NOT pairs!) ***from fabric strips facing RIGHT SIDE UP***. *[Step 3]* • Cut (4) 3" strips; cut (52) 3" x 3" squares. *[Step 2]*
Fabric #7 Medium	¾ yard	• Cut (8) 2½" strips and piece together for the inner borders. (Optional: See Step 5.)
Backing	4 yards	• 2 panels 36" x 72"
Batting		• 72" x 72"
Binding	¾ yard	• Cut (8) 2¼" strips. Join end-to-end.

Step 1: Construct the Flying Geese Units

- Refer to pages 16 & 17 for directions to make 52 flying geese units using:
  - 104 (52 pairs) fabric #3 B triangles
  - 52 (20) fabric #2 A triangles
- Press the seams toward the side triangles. The units should measure 3" x 5½" unfinished. Square up if necessary.

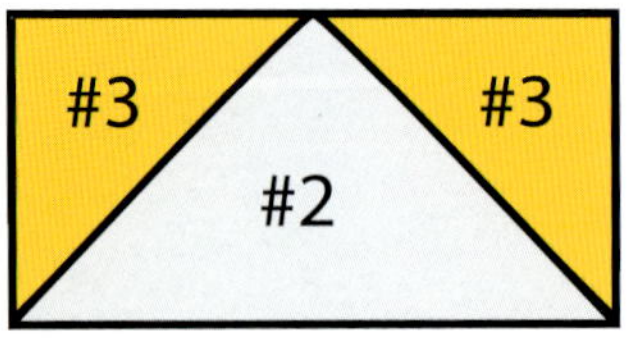

Make 52.

Step 2: Construct the Sawtooth Star Blocks

- For each block you will need:
  - 4 – fabric #2/#3 flying geese units
  - 1 – fabric #3 – 5½" squares
  - 4 – fabric #6 – 3" squares
- Assemble 13 Sawtooth Star blocks as shown. The blocks should measure 10½" x 10½" unfinished. Square up if necessary.

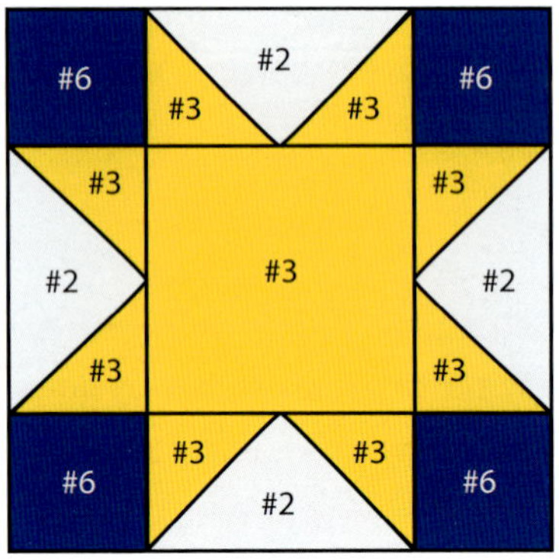

Make 13.

Step 3: Construct the Pinwheel Blocks

- Make 96 flying geese units using:
  - 48 – fabric #2 Side A triangles
  - 48 – fabric #4 Side A triangles
  - 96 – fabric #2 Side B triangles
  - 48 – fabric #5 Side B triangles (right side)
  - 48 – fabric #6 Side B triangles (left side)
- Press the seams toward the side triangles. The units should measure 3" x 5½" unfinished. Square up if necessary.

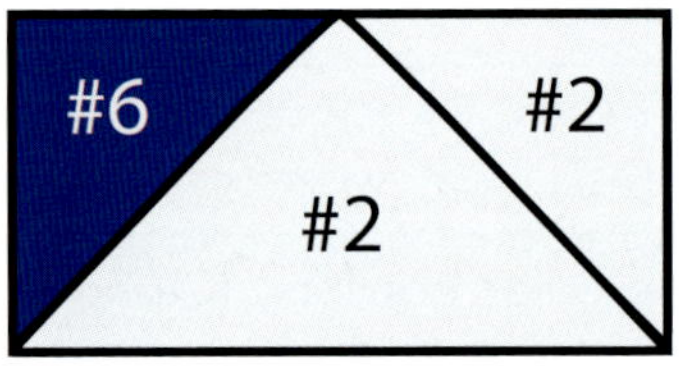

Make 48 flying geese units as shown. Follow the diagram carefully. You will sew a fabric #2 wing unit to the right side of a fabric #2 geese unit.

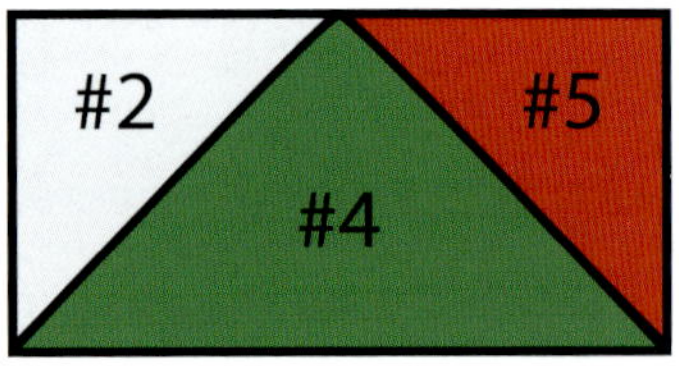

Make 48 flying geese units as shown.

Step 4: Construct the Pinwheel Blocks

- For each block, you will need:
  - 4 fabric #6/#2/#2 flying geese units
  - 4 fabric #2/#4/#5 flying geese units
- Make 12 Pinwheel blocks as shown.
- The blocks should measure 10½" x 10½" unfinished.
- Square up if necessary.

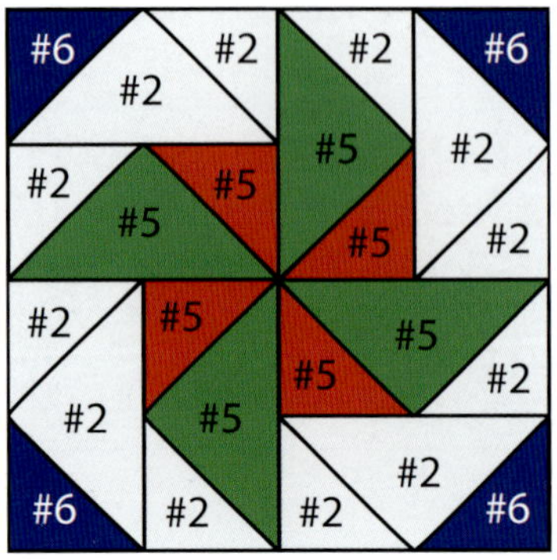

Make 12.

Step 5: Quilt Top Assembly

- Alternate the Pinwheel and Sawtooth Star blocks as shown in the diagram.
- Add the inner and outer borders to the quilt. NOTE: For a more modern aesthetic, don't use borders at all. Use a simple block layout and quilt as desired.

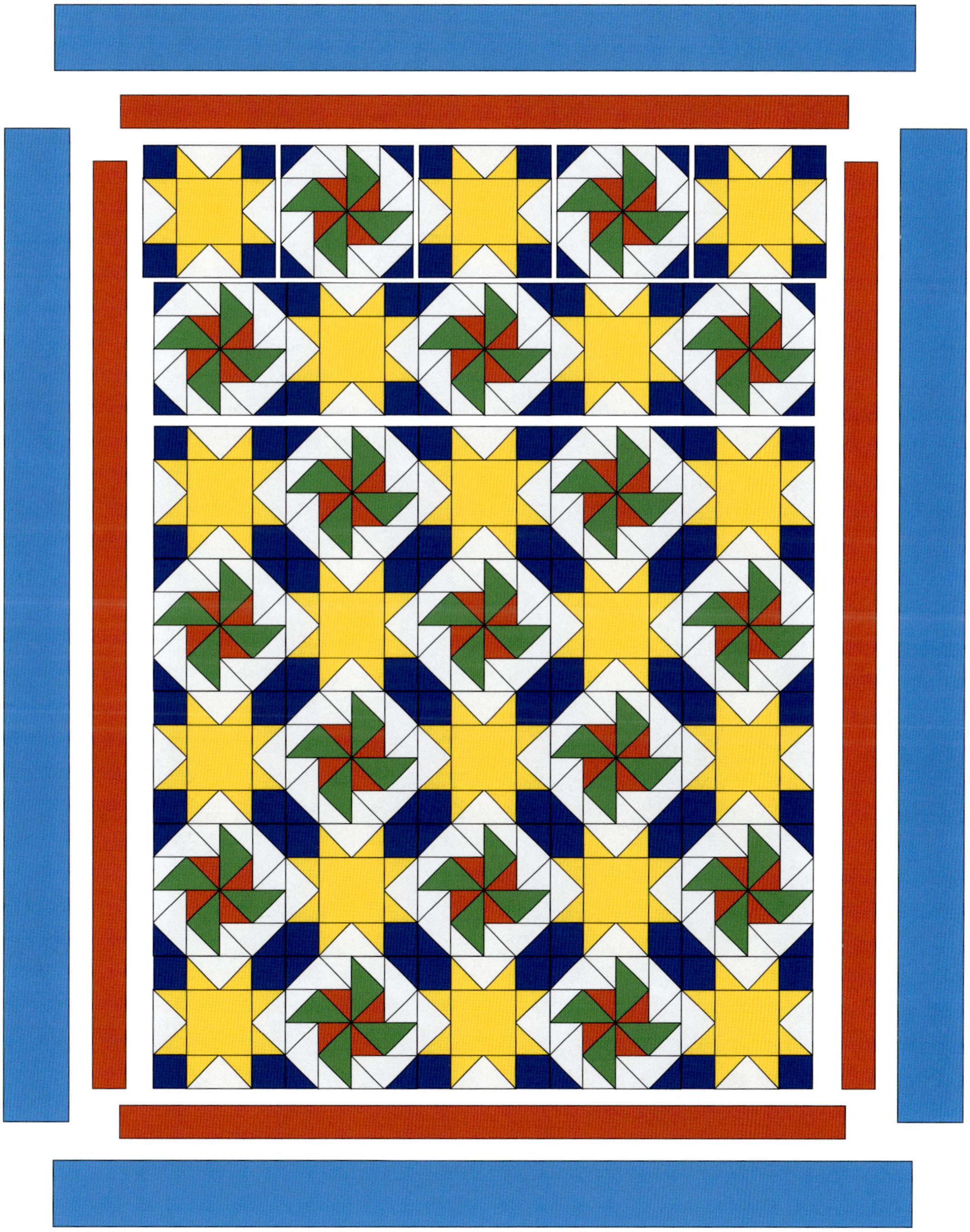

Quilt assembly

Layout Options

Try this easy layout of 8 blocks across by 9 blocks down, sans borders, for a bold, masculine and dynamic look. You will need a total of 72 blocks—36 Sawtooth Star blocks and 36 Pinwheel blocks. The quilt will measure 80" x 90".

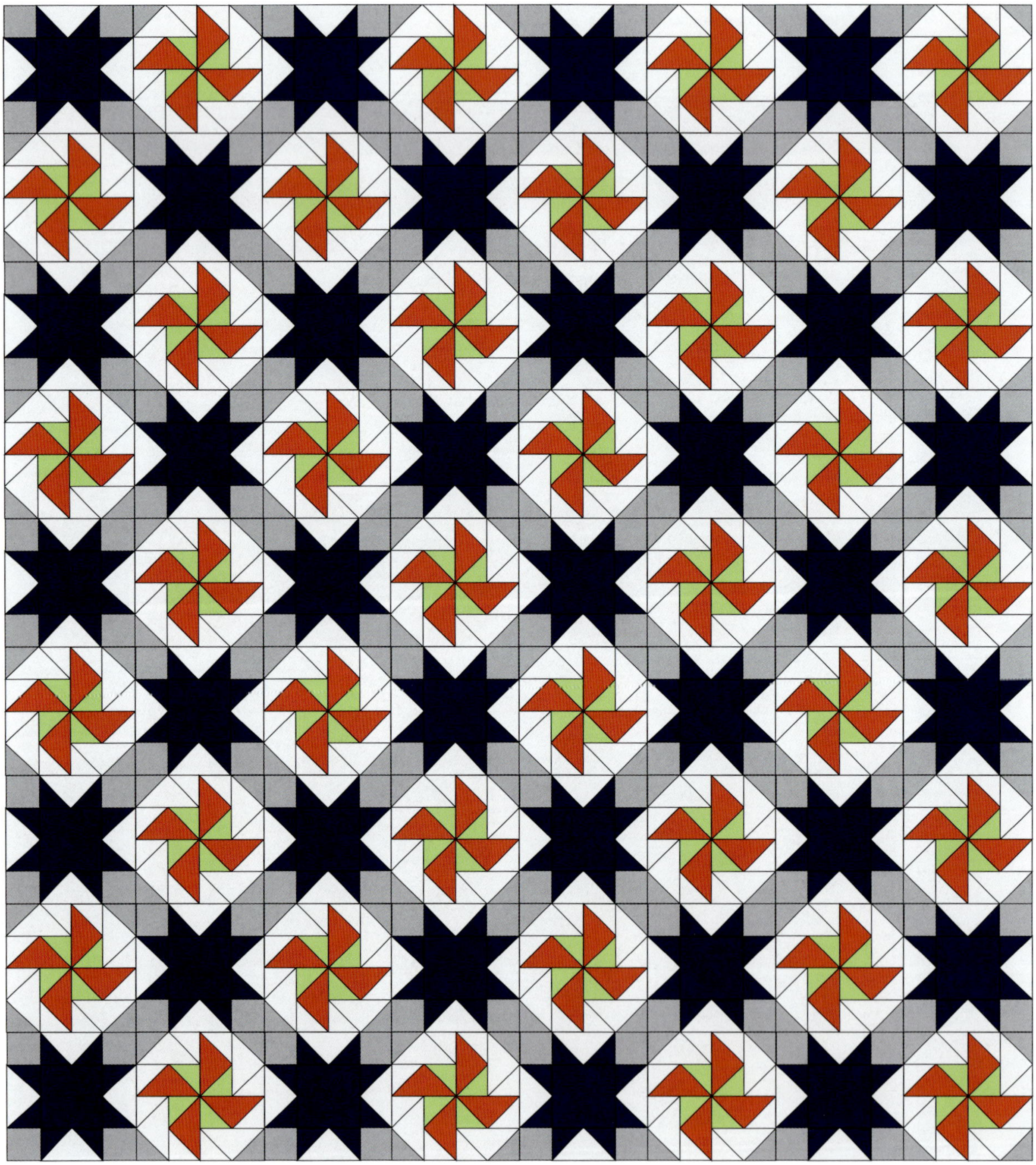

You may want to try this double/queen size version, which measures 96" x 96", with an inner and outer border added. It looks lovely in a soft, muted, romantic colorway. You will need a total of 64 blocks—32 Sawtooth Star blocks and 32 Pinwheel blocks.

STAR FLIGHT, 48" x 48", designed and made by the author; quilted by Birgit Schüller, Riegelsberg, Germany, Cretive BiTS

Star Flight

Quilt size: 48" x 48"

Finished block sizes: 24" x 24" and 8" x 8"

Skill level: Skilled Beginner

Star Flight might just be one of my most favorite designs. *Ever*. It has all of my favorite elements, cleverly combined. As I was working on the design for this quilt and I arrived at this layout for the blocks using my EQ software, I just *knew*. Perfection. Everything just "clicked." I liked it so much, I decided to make it – multiple times! And this quilt looks spectacular done in both light and dark background versions, so take your pick. It will look wonderful whether you choose batiks or print fabrics. Modern or reproduction. This is a winner no matter how your geese take flight!

Fabric Requirements and Cutting Instructions

• Cut all strips across the WOF (selvage to selvage).

FABRIC	YARDS	INSTRUCTIONS
Fabric #1 Light Background	1¾ yards	• Cut (1) 6½" strip; use the ***EZ Flying Geese Ruler*** to cut 4 **Side A** triangles. *[Step 3]* • Cut (2) 4½" strips; use the ***EZ Flying Geese Ruler*** to cut 24 **Side B** triangle PAIRS. *[Step 7]* • Cut (2) 4½" strips; subcut (16) 4½" square. *[Step 2]* • Cut (4) 2½" strips. *[Step 1]* • Cut (3) 4½" strips; subcut (8) 4½" x 8½" rectangles and (8) 4½" squares. *[Step 8]* • Cut (1) 2½" strip; cut it in half so each piece is approximately 20" in length. *[Step 5]* • Cut (1) 4½" strip; cut it in half and use one piece approximately 20" in length. *[Step 5]*
Fabric #2 Light	½ yard	• Cut (2) 4½" strips; subcut into (8) 4½" squares for the Chain blocks. *[Step 2]* and (8) 4½" squares *[for the border blocks]*. • Cut (1) 6½" strip; subcut into (1) 6½" square. Trim the remainder to 3½". • From the remaining 3½" strips; use the ***EZ Flying Geese Ruler*** to cut 4 **Side B** triangle PAIRS. *[Step 3]*
Fabric #3 Medium light	⅝ yard	• Cut (2) 2½" strips. *[Step 1]* • Cut (5) 2¼" strips for binding. Join end-to-end.
Fabric #4 Medium	⅓ yard	• Cut (2) 4½" strips; use the ***EZ Flying Geese Ruler*** to cut 12 **Side A** triangles. *[Step 7]*

(continued)

(continued)

FABRIC	YARDS	INSTRUCTIONS
Fabric #5 Medium dark	½ yard	• Cut (1) 6½" strip; use the ***EZ Flying Geese Ruler*** to cut 4 **Side B** triangle PAIRS. *[Step 3]* • Cut (1) 3½" strip; cut (4) 3½" squares and 4 **Side A** triangles. *[Step 3]*
Fabric #6 Dark	⅓ yard	• Cut (1) 2½" strip; cut it in half so each piece is approximately 20" in length. *[Step 5]* • Cut (2) 2½" strips. *[Step 1]*
Backing	3¼ yards	

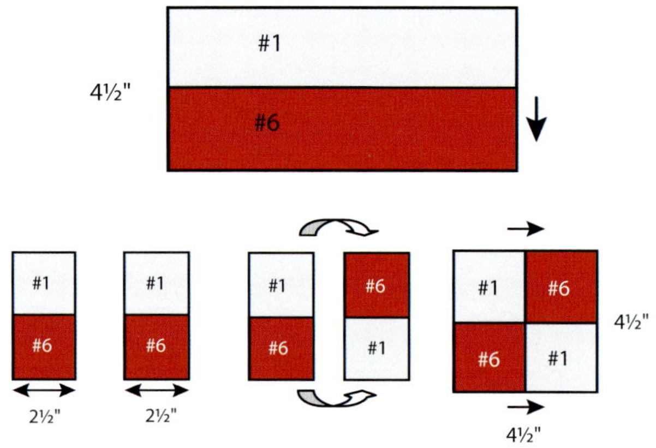

Make 2 strip-sets. Cut 24 - 2½" segments.

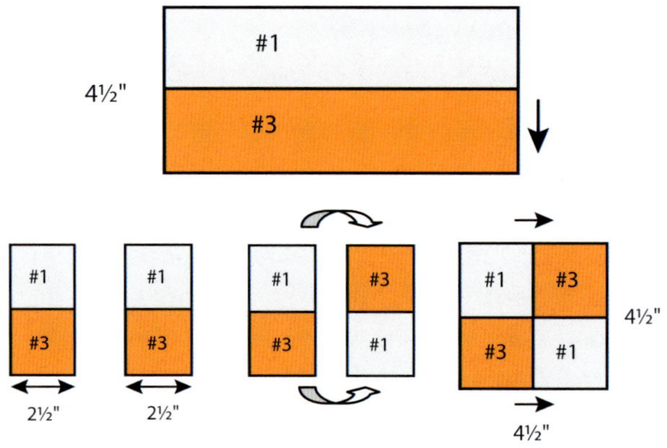

Make 2 strip-sets. Cut 32 - 2½" segments.

Dark Background Version

For a dark background version, simply reverse the values of the fabrics; fabric #1 should be the dark background, fabric #2, the darkest, and fabric #6 the lightest.

Step 1: Construct the Four-Patch Units

- Sew 2½" strips of fabrics #1 and #6 into a strip-set as shown.
- Press the seam closed first, then press unit open with seam toward darker fabric.
- Repeat to make a total of 2 strip-sets.
- Cut 24 – 2½" segments.
- Join 2 segments to make a four-patch unit. Press the seam to one side.
- Make 12 four-patch units. The units should measure 4½" x 4½" (unfinished). Square up if necessary.
- Repeat the process using 2½" strips of fabrics #1 and #3. Make 2 strip-sets.
- Cut 32 – 2½" segments as shown.
- Make 16 four-patch units. The units should measure 4½" x 4 ½" (unfinished). Square up if necessary.

Step 2: Construct the Chain Blocks

- Use 16 – 4½" squares of fabric #1 plus the 16 fabric #1/#3 four-patch units to assemble the Chain blocks as shown.
- Press the seams away from the four-patch units.
- Make 8 Chain blocks. The blocks should measure 8½" x 8½" (unfinished). Square up if necessary.
- Repeat the process, using 8 – 4½" squares of fabric

#2 plus the 8 fabric #1/#6 four-patch units to assemble the Chain blocks as shown.

- Press the seams away from the four-patch units.
- Make 4 Chain blocks. The blocks should measure 8½" x 8½" (unfinished). Square up if necessary.

Step 3: Construct the Flying Geese Units

- Refer to pages 16 & 17 for directions to make 4 flying geese units using:
  - 8 fabric #2 B triangles
  - 4 fabric #5 A triangles
- Press the seams away from the center triangle.
- The flying geese units should measure 3" x 6" unfinished. Square up if necessary.

- Make 4 large flying geese units using:
  - 8 fabric #5 B triangles
  - 4 fabric #1 A triangles
- Press the seams away from the center triangle.
- The flying geese units should measure 3" x 6" unfinished. Square up if necessary.

Step 4: Partially Assemble the Star-in-a-Star Block

- Use 4 – 3½" fabric #5 squares, one 6½" fabric #2 square, and the 4 small flying geese units to construct the inner Sawtooth Star as shown.
- The block should measure 12½" x 12½" (unfinished). Square up if necessary.
- Add 2 large flying geese units to the sides of the inner Sawtooth Star block as shown in the completed block figure on page 52.
- Press the seams toward the large flying geese units.
- Set aside the remaining 2 large flying geese units for the moment; do not complete the assembly yet.

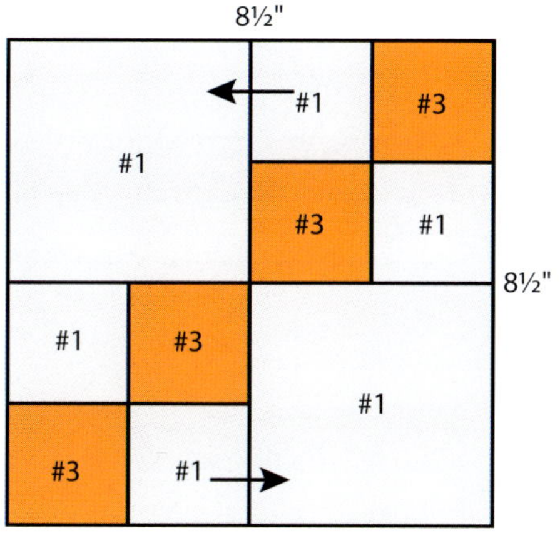

Make 8.

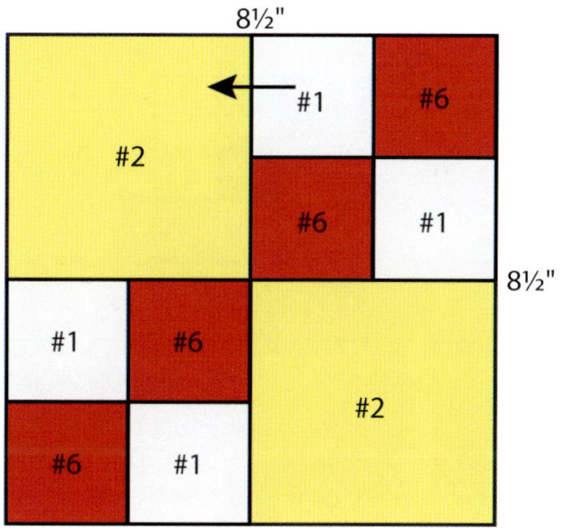

Make 4.

Make 4.

Make 4.

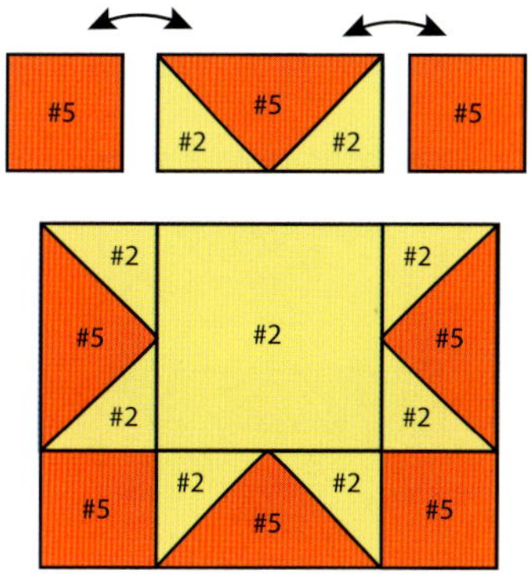

Step 5: Construct the Nine-Patch Variation Units

- Join a 20" – 2½" fabric #6 strip and 2 – 20" – 2½" fabric #1 strips to make a strip-set as shown.
- Press the seams away from fabric #6.
- Cut 4 – 2½" segments.
- Join a 20" – 2½" fabric #6 strip and a 20" – 4½" fabric #1 strip to make a strip-set as shown.
- Press the seams away from fabric #6.
- Cut 8 – 2½" segments.
- Sew a #1/#6/#1 segment between 2 - #6/#1 segments as shown.
- Make 4 nine-patch variation units as shown.

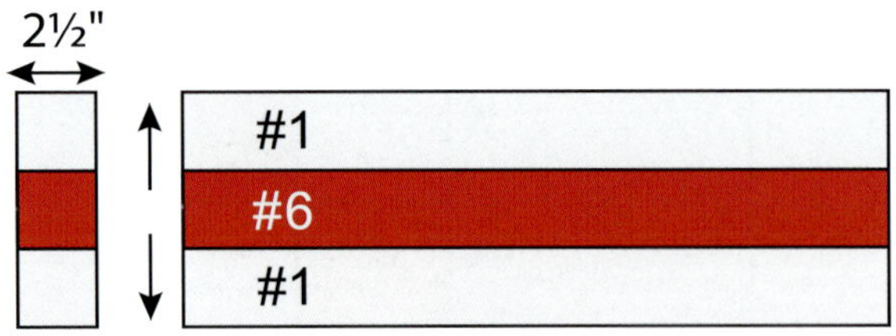

Cut 4. *Make 1.*

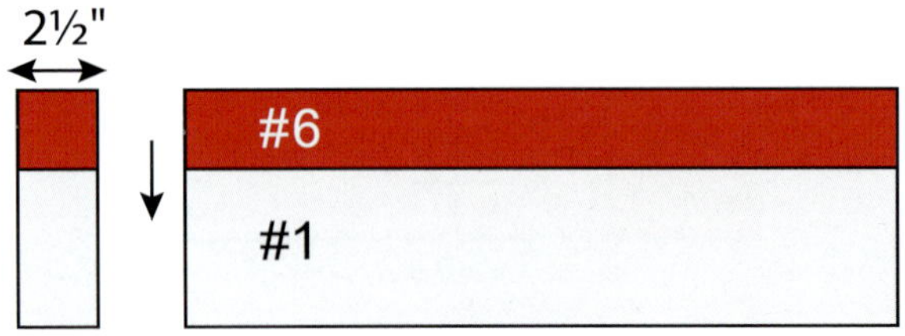

Cut 8. *Make 1.*

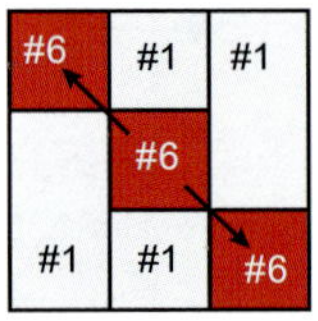

Make 4.

Step 6: Complete the Star-in-a-Star Block

- Add a nine-patch variation unit to each end of the remaining large flying geese units.
- Add to the partially assembled block.
- Press the seams toward the nine-patch variation units.
- The Star-in-a-Star block should measure 24½" x 24½" (unfinished). Square up if necessary, but be sure to leave seam allowance at the points.

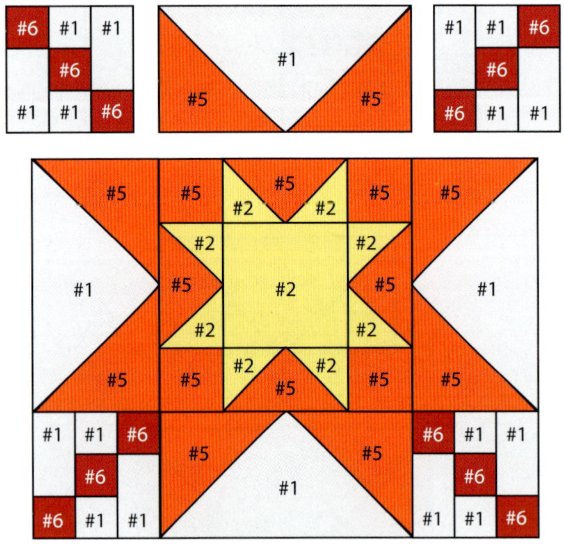

Step 7: Construct Double-Flying Geese Blocks

- Refer to pages 16 & 17 for directions to make 12 flying geese units using:
  - 24 fabric #1 B triangles
  - 12 fabric #4 A triangles
- Press the seams away from the center triangle.
- The flying geese units should measure 4½" x 8½" (unfinished). Square up if necessary.
- Join 2 flying geese units to complete each Double-Flying Geese block as shown.
- Make 4 blocks. The blocks should measure 8½" x 8½". Square up if necessary.
- Set aside the remaining 4 flying geese units for the pieced outer border.

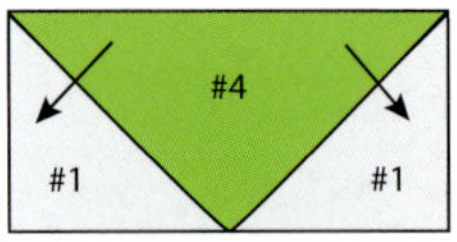

Make 12.

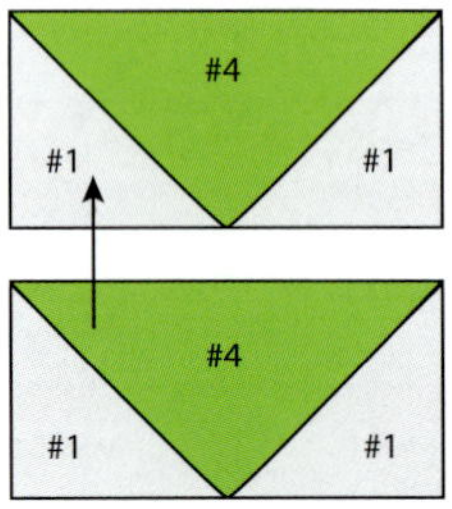

Make 4.

Step 8: Assemble the Quilt Top

- Add a fabric #1/#3 Chain block to both sides of 2 Double-Flying Geese blocks, paying careful attention to the orientation of each of the blocks.
- Add to the sides of the Star-in-a-Star block.
- Add a fabric #1/#3 Chain block and a fabric #1/#6 Chain block to both sides of the remaining Double-Flying Geese blocks, again paying attention to the orientation of the blocks.
- Add to the top and bottom to complete the quilt top.

Step 9: Pieced Border Assembly

- Join the remaining flying geese units, strip-set segments, and fabric #1 rectangles as shown to construct the side and top and bottom pieced borders as shown to extend the design into the borders.
- The quilt top should measure 48½" x 48½" (unfinished).
- Baste, quilt as desired, bind, add label (be sure to use permanent ink!) and ENJOY!

Quilt assembly

Dark layout option

Zen

Designed by the author; made by Claire Neal, Hampton Roads, VA; quilted by Birgit Schüller, Riegelsberg, Germany, Creative BiTS

Once I made the light background version, Star Flight, I was eager to try the design with a dark background. The batik colors blended beautifully, but the machine quilted motifs gave this design a truly oriental feel! Like Star Flight, the lack of an outer border gives this a clean, crisp, modern feel.

Hot Nights

Designed by the author; made by Claire Neal, Hampton Roads, VA; quilted by Carolyn Archer, Ohio Star Quilting

These fabrics were a fun and vibrant starting point for a quilt that reminds me of hot summer nights and neon lights! It boldly demonstrates that you can just as easily use print fabrics, rather than batiks, to make this design really sparkle!

Tropical Fish

Designed by the author; made by Claire Neal, Hampton Roads, VA; quilted by Carolyn Archer, Ohio Star Quilting

The tropical fish batik print was the inspiration for this version. And since I wanted this version to have more of a traditional feel, I added the outer borders so it feels less modern.

SPRING CABIN FEVER, 46" x 46", designed by the author; made by Linda Baxter Lasco, Sunapee, NH; quilted by Carolyn Archer, Ohio Star Quilting

Spring Cabin Fever

Quilt size: 46" x 46"

Finished block sizes: 20" x 20" and 10" x 10"

Skill level: Intermediate

This quilt holds a special place in my heart. I actually designed it using four different blocks to commemorate a special anniversary for the long-running Vermont Quilt Festival and also to celebrate the purchase of our quaint little vacation cabin tucked away in the mountains. The names of the blocks came easily to me. I chose a traditional Log Cabin block, a Pine Tree block, and I combined a Bear Paw and Ohio Star block for the center. I absolutely love the secondary star created by the Log Cabin blocks! This was such a fun quilt to make, too. Once the cutting is done, the unit construction and block assembly goes quite quickly. Whether you fancy a holiday in the mountains or the beach, I think you'll love making this pretty quilted wallhanging for your home or someone special.

Fabric Requirements and Cutting Instructions

• Cut all strips across the WOF (selvage to selvage).

FABRIC	YARDS	INSTRUCTIONS
Fabric #1 Light Background	1¾ yards	• Cut (3) 2½" strips. *[Step 1]* • Cut (1) 2½" strip; subcut (16) 2½" x 2½" squares. *[Steps 2 & 3]* • Cut (1) 3½" strip. *[Step 2]* • Cut (1) 6" strip; subcut (2) 6" squares. Cut the squares 2x diagonally to yield 8 triangles. *[Step 3]* • Cut (10) 1½" strips; cut the following rectangles: *[Step 4]* (8) 1½" x 9½" (8) 1½" x 8½" (8) 1½" x 7½" (8) 1½" x 6½" (8) 1½" x 5½" (8) 1½" x 4½" (8) 1½" x 3½" (8) 1½" x 2½" • Cut (2) 1½" strips; subcut the following rectangles: *[Step 2]* (2) 1½" x 20½" (2) 1½" x 18½" • Cut (4) 3½" strips. *[Step 5]*

(continued)

(continued)

FABRIC	YARDS	INSTRUCTIONS
Fabric #2 Medium light	½ yard	• Cut (1) 2½" strip. *[Step 1]* • Cut (1) 4½" strip; subcut (4) 4½" x 4½" squares. *[Step 2]* • (1) 2½" strip; subcut (5) 2½" x 2½" squares. *[Step 2]*
Fabric #3 Medium	½ yard	• Cut (1) 3½" strip; subcut (4) 3½" squares. *[Step 5]* Set aside the remainder of strip. *[Step 2]* • Cut (1) 2½" strip; subcut (12) 2½" x 2½" squares. *[Steps 2 & 4]*
Fabric #4 Medium dark	½ yard	• Cut (2) 2½" strips. *[Step 1]* • Cut (1) 6½" strip. *[Step 3]*
Fabric #5 Dark or Main, Multicolor (Focus Fabric)	1½ yards (Includes Binding)	• Cut (1) 3½" strip. *[Step 2]* • Cut (12) 1½" strips; cut the following rectangles: *[Step 4]* (8) 1½" x 10½" (8) 1½" x 9½" (8) 1½" x 8½" (8) 1½" x 7½" (8) 1½" x 6½" (8) 1½" x 5½" (8) 1½" x 4½" (8) 1½" x 3½" (8) 1½" x 2½" • Cut (5) 2½" strips; join end-to-end for the binding.
Backing	3½ yards	• 2 panels 26" x 52" and piece for the backing
Batting		• 52" x 52"

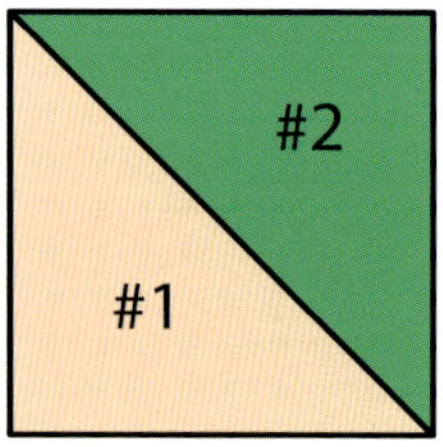

Make 16.

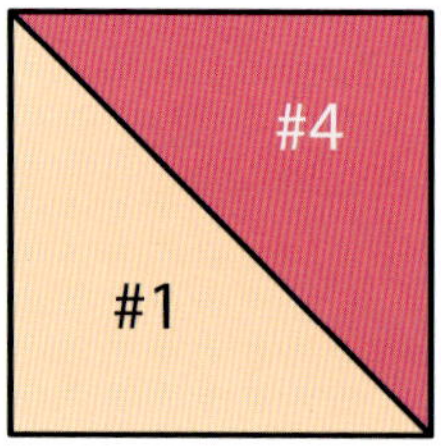

Make 56.

Step 1: Construct the HSTs

- Place the fabric #1 and fabric #2 – 2½" strips RST.
- Use Side B of the EZ Flying Geese Ruler to cut 16 – 2½" triangle PAIRS. Refer to page 16 for directions to cut, sew, and trim the triangle units to make 16 HSTs. Press the seam allowance toward the darker fabric.
- The HSTs should measure 2½" x 2½" unfinished. Square up if necessary.
- Repeat the process with (2) 2½" strips each of fabrics #1 and #4 to make 56 HSTs.

Step 2: Construct the Star Block Units

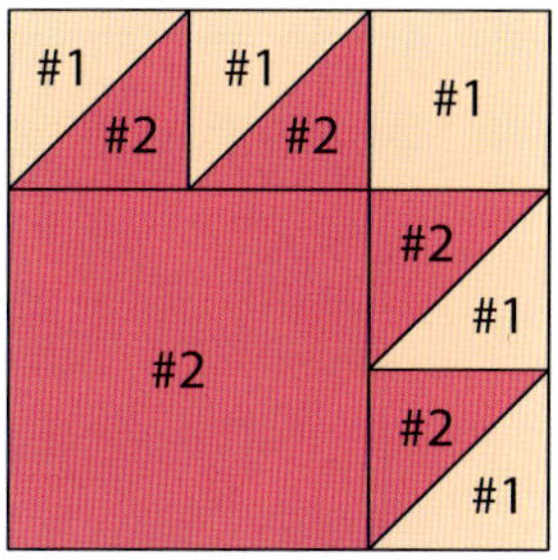

- Use the following to construct the nine-patch unit:
  - 5 – 2½" x 2½" squares of fabric #2
  - 4 – 2½" x 2½" squares of fabric #3
- Press the seams toward fabric #3.
- The unit should measure 6½" x 6½" square. Square up if necessary.
- Make 1.

- Use the following to construct each Bear Paw unit:
  - 4 – 2½" fabrics #1/#2 HSTs
  - 1 – 4½" x 4½" square of fabric #2
  - 1 – 2½" x 2½" square of fabric #1
- Make 4.
- The units should measure 6½" x 6½" square. Square up if necessary.

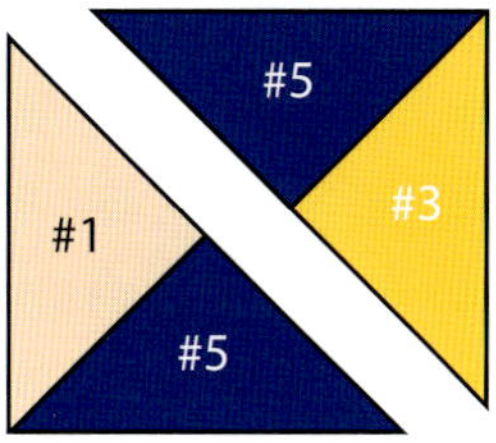

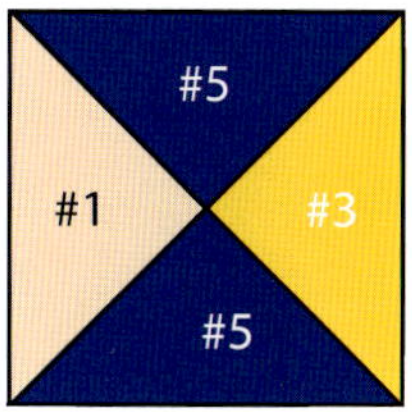

- Use 3½" strips of fabrics #1, #3, and #5 to construct the quad-triangle units:
  - Use Side A of the EZ Flying Geese Ruler to cut 4 triangles from fabrics #1 and #3 and 8 triangles from fabric #5.
  - Join them as shown to construct the quad-triangle units.
- Make 4. Press the seams toward fabric #5 but press middle seam open.
- The units should measure 6½" x 6½". Square up if necessary.

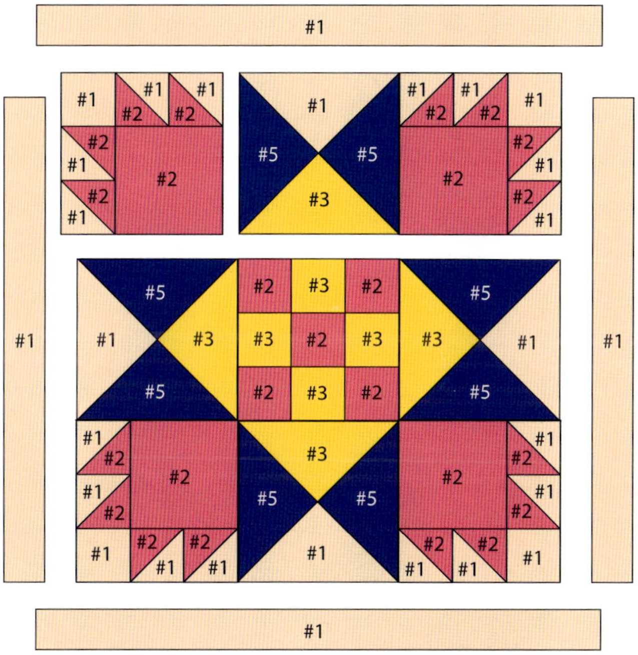

- Join the units in a nine-patch configuration to make the Star block as shown.
- The block should measure 18½" x 18½" (unfinished). Square up if necessary.
- Add the following fabric #1 strips to the sides, top and bottom to complete the center block.
  - 2 – 1½" x 18½" rectangles
  - 2 – 1½" x 20½" rectangles
- Press the seams toward fabric #1.
- The final block should measure 20½" x 20½" (unfinished).

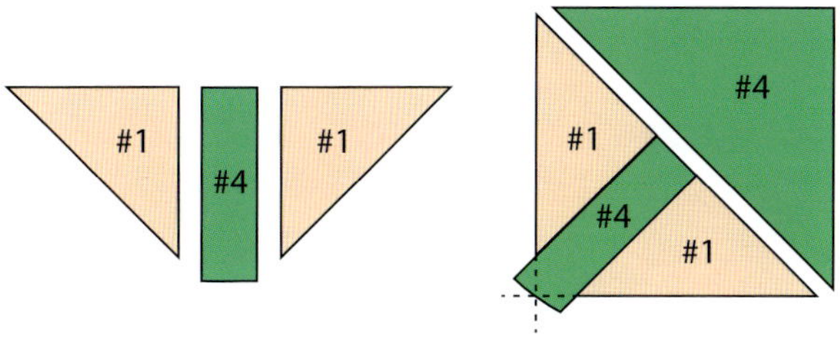

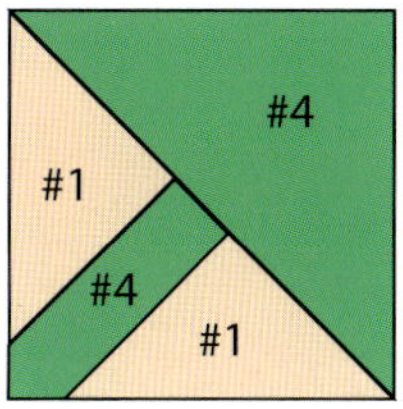

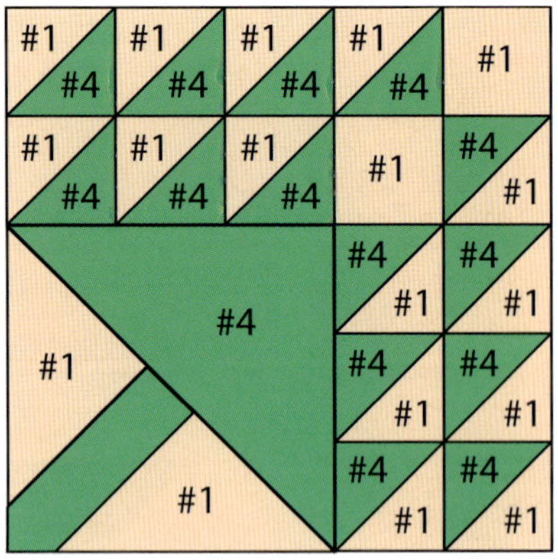

Step 3: Construct the Tree Trunk Unit

- Use the ***EZ Flying Geese Ruler*** to cut 4 Side B triangles from the 6½" strip of fabric #4.
- Trim the remaining strip to 5½". Cut (4) 2¼" x 5½" rectangles.
- Stitch the rectangle between two fabric #1 triangles cut from the 6" squares.
- Sew fabric #4 Side B triangles to complete the tree trunk units as shown on page 59. Square up the unit to measure 6½" x 6½" (unfinished).
- Use the following to construct each Vermont Pine Tree block:
  - 14 – 2½" fabrics #1/#4 HSTs
  - 2 – 2½" x 2½" squares of fabric #1
  - 1 tree trunk unit
- Make 4.
- The blocks should measure 10½" x 10½" square (unfinished). Square up if necessary.

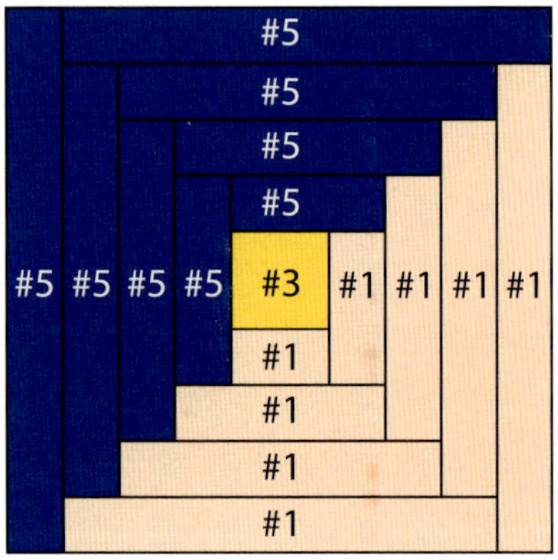

Step 4: Construct the Log Cabin Blocks

- Start with a 2½" x 2½" square of fabric #3.
- Beginning with the shortest fabric #1 – 1½" rectangle, add to a side of the square. Add the next size fabric #1 rectangle to the adjacent side.
- Add 2 fabric #5 rectangles as shown, again starting with the shortest.
- Continue, alternating adding the next 2 sizes of fabrics #1 & #5 to complete the block as shown.
- Press the seams away from the center square after each addition.
- Make 8. The blocks should measure 10½" x 10 ½" (unfinished). Square up if necessary.

Quilt assembly

Step 5: Construct the Quilt Top

- Lay out the blocks as shown for a large star design or as shown in the quilt photo (page 56) for a center diamond.
- Join the blocks into rows; sew the rows together.
- Add the fabric #1 – 3½" strips and the fabric #3 – 3½" squares as cornerstones for the outer border.

Cabin Fever

Designed and made by the author, quilted by Carolyn Archer, Ohio Star Quilting

The first thing you'll notice about this version is the green color in the Log Cabin blocks instead of the background color. The truth is, I ran out of background fabric and didn't have enough to make the quilt top, so I improvised! I had extra green fabric so I used what I had on hand. It gives the quilt a different look and makes me happy to know that I made do without worrying about finding more of that elusive background fabric. And I love the way it looks over the mantle in our little cabin. Comfy, cozy, and perfect!

Bonus Layout:

This quilt would be lovely made larger simply by making more blocks (16 Pine Tree, 16 Bear Paw, and 32 Log Cabin, total). And just think how classic it would look as a two-color option, such as the classic red and white!

GLACIER BAY, 54" x 54", designed and made by the author; quilted by Carolyn Archer, Ohio Star Quilting

GLACIER BAY

Quilt size: 54" x 54"

Finished block sizes: 18" x 18" and 9" x 9"

Skill level: Intermediate

I've been blessed to teach on many quilting cruises—three times to Alaska. The scenery was stunning and to top it off, it felt as though we were shop-hopping from the ship because there was at least one quilt shop in every port of call! My favorite day on board, though, was always when we went to see the glacier calving. The wonder of seeing the large, imposing ice formations was both awe-inspiring and breathtaking. I designed this quilt as a mystery quilt for one of those cruises and I used batiks I found in those Alaskan quilt shops to make the quilt.

I used some leftover fabrics and cut 3½" squares to make some Prairie Points. I randomly placed them between the middle and outer borders. I just love how they lend a rugged, ragged feel of the fractured ice we saw on those glaciers. However, as you'll see in the Spring color version, you don't need Alaskan fabrics to make this design really sparkle. Choose any fabrics and watch this design twinkle and shine!

Fabric Requirements and Cutting Instructions

• Cut all strips across the WOF (selvage to selvage).

FABRIC	YARDS	INSTRUCTIONS
Fabric #1 Light-Cream Background	1 yard	• Cut (1) 3" strip; subcut (4) 3" x 3" squares. *[Step 5]* • Cut (2) 3" strips. *[Step 1]* • Cut (2) 3½" strips; subcut (8) 3½" x 6½" rectangles. *[Step 4]* • Cut (3) 3½" strip; subcut (24) 3½" squares. *[Step 4]* • Cut (1) 1½" strip. *[Step 2]* • Cut (1) 2½" strip. *[Step 2]* • Cut (1) 2" strip. *[Step 3]*
Fabric #2 Multicolor print Gold/Purple	⅝ yard	• Cut (1) 3½" strip. *[Step 1]* • Cut (1) 3½" strip; subcut (1) 3½" x 3½" square. *[Step 5]*. • Set aside the remaining strip for HSTs. *[Step 1]* • Cut (4) 3½" strips for inner border.
Fabric #3 Medium Plum	⅝ yard	• Cut (1) 5½" strip; subcut (4) 5½" x 5½" squares. *[Step 5]* • Trim the remaining strip to 3½" and cut (4) 3½" x 3½" squares. *[Step 4]* • Cut (2) 3" strips. *[Step 1]* • Cut (5) 2½" strips. Piece as needed for the middle border.

(continued)

(continued)

FABRIC	YARDS	INSTRUCTIONS
Fabric #4 Medium light Aqua	1 yard	• Cut (1) 3½" strip; subcut (8) 3½" x 3½" squares. *[Step 4]* • Cut (3) 1½" strips. *[Step 2]* • Cut (1) 2" strip. *[Step 3]* • Cut (6) 2¼" strips for the binding. Join end-to-end.
Fabric #5 Medium dark Purple	⅓ yard	• Cut (2) 2" strips. *[Step 3]*
Fabric #6 Dark Black Print	½ yard	• Cut (1) 3½" strip. *[Step 1]* • Cut (5) 4½" strips for the outer border. • Cut (1) 3½" strip; subcut (4) 3½" x 8" rectangles. *[Step 5]* • Cut (2) 3½" strips; subcut (16) 3½" x 3½" squares. *[Step 4]* • Cut (1) 1½" strip. *[Step 2]* • Cut (1) 2½" strip. *[Step 2]*
Backing	3½ yards	• Cut 2 panels 30" x 60" and piece for the backing.
Batting		• 2 panels 28" x 54"

Make 16.

Make 4.

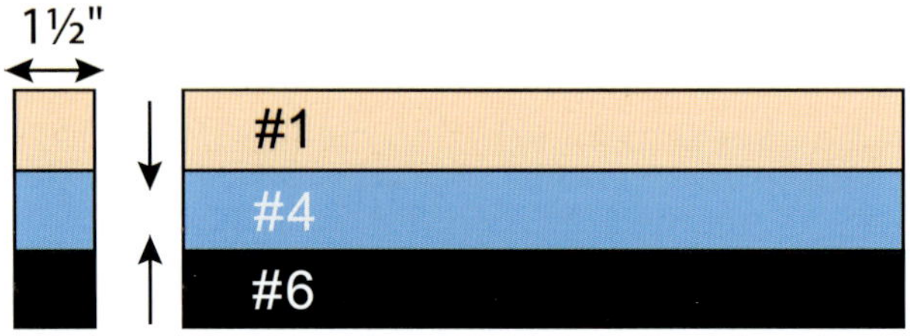

Cut 16. *Make 1.*

Step 1: Construct the HSTs

- Place the fabric #1 and fabric #3 – 3" strips RST.
- Use **Side B** of the ***EZ Flying Geese Ruler*** to cut (16) 3" triangle PAIRS. Refer to page 16 for directions to cut, sew, and trim the triangle units to make 16 HSTs. Press the seam allowance toward the darker fabric.
- The HSTs should measure 3" x 3" unfinished. Square up if necessary.
- Place the fabric #2 and fabric #6 – 3½" strips RST.
- Use **Side B** of the ***EZ Flying Geese Ruler*** to cut (8) 3½" triangle PAIRS. Make 8 HSTs. Press the seam allowance toward the darker fabric.
- The HSTs should measure 3½" x 3½" (unfinished). Square up if necessary.

Step 2: Construct the Chain Blocks

- Sew 1½" strips of fabrics #1, #4, and #6 into a strip set as shown. Press the seams toward fabric #4.
- Cut 16 – 1½" segments.

- Sew a fabric #4 – 1½" strip and a fabric #1 – 2½" strip into a strip-set. Press the seams toward fabric #4.
- Cut 16 – 1½" segments.
- Sew a fabric #4 – 1½" strip and a fabric #6 – 2½" strip into a strip-set. Press the seams toward fabric #1.
- Cut 16 – 1½" segments.
- Sew the segments into Chain blocks as shown. Press the seams away from the center.
- Make 16.
- The blocks should measure 3½" square (unfinished). Square up if necessary.

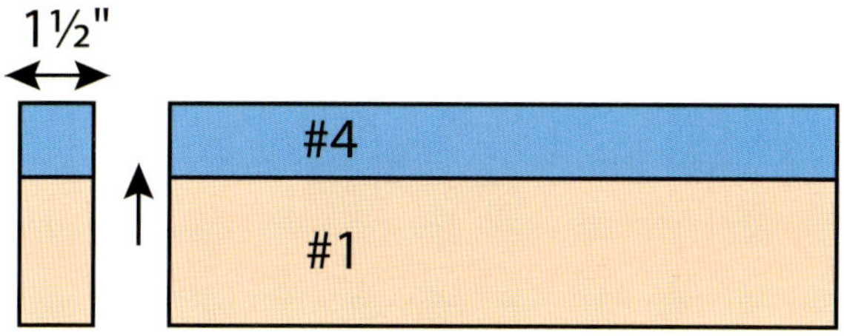

Cut 16. *Make 1.*

Cut 16. *Make 1.*

Step 3: Construct the Quad-Triangle Units

Use **Side A** of the ***EZ Flying Geese Ruler*** to cut 64 (total) A triangles from the following 2" strips.

- Fabric #1 - Cut 16 from 1 – 2" strip.
- Fabric #4 - Cut 16 from 1 – 2" strip.
- Fabric #5 - Cut 32 from 2 – 2" strips.

- Lay out the triangles as shown.
- Sew the triangles together. Press the seams toward the fabric #5 triangles.
- Make 16. Square up the units to measure 3½" square (unfinished).

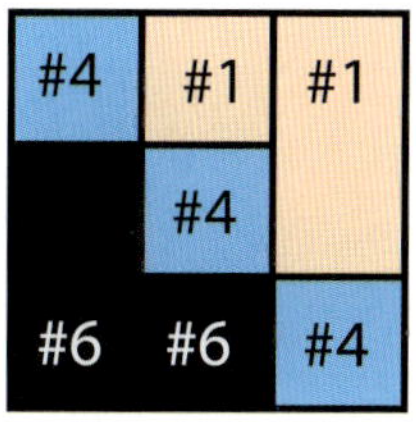

Make 16.

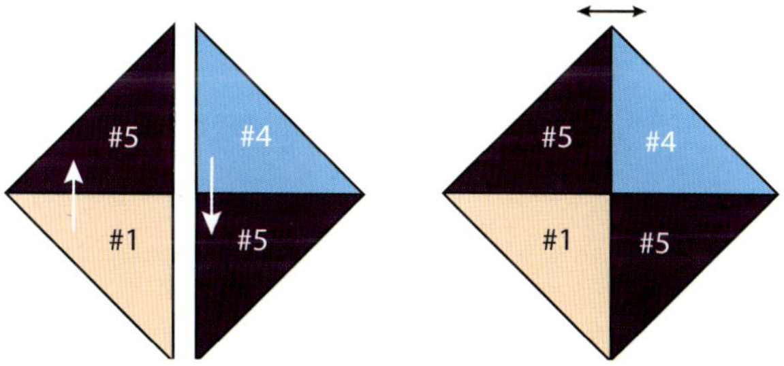

Make 16.

Step 4: Assemble the Glacier Blocks

- For each Glacier block use:
  - 1 – fabric #1 – 3½" square
  - 1 – fabric #1 – 3½" x 6½" rectangle
  - 2 – fabric #6 – 3½" squares
  - 1 – fabric #4 – 3½" square
  - 1 – fabric #2/#6 – 3½" HST
  - 2 – 3½" Chain blocks
- Carefully follow the placement of the pieced units as shown.
- Follow the arrows to press the seams.
- Make 8. The blocks should measure 9½" square (unfinished).
- Square up if necessary.

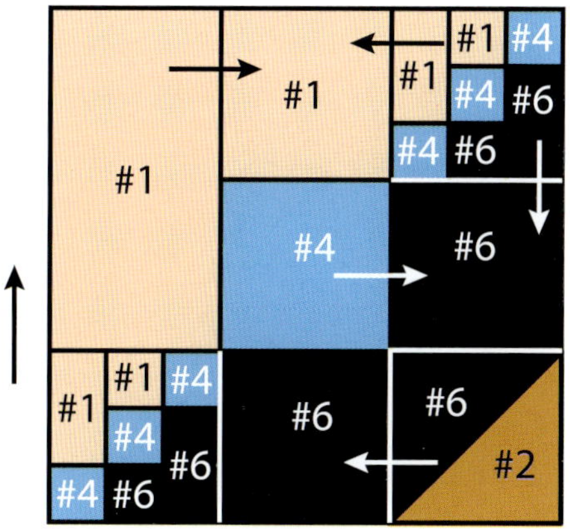

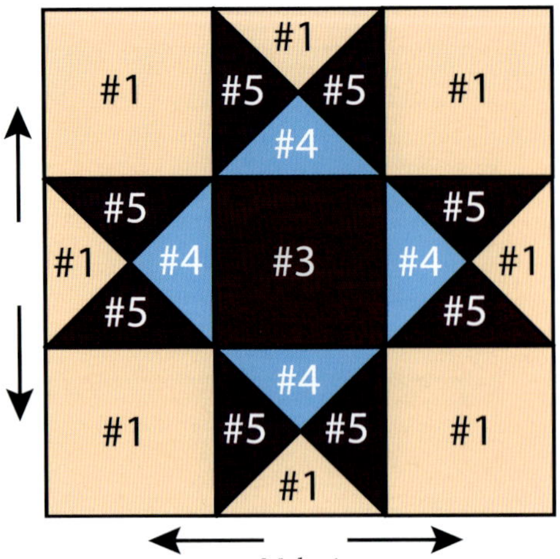

Make 4.

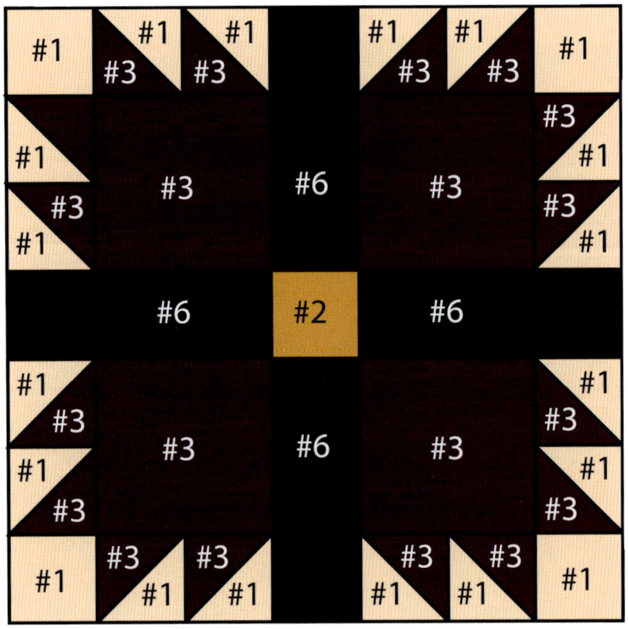

Make 4.

Step 5: Assemble the Northern Star Blocks

- For each Northern Star block use:
  - 4 – fabric #1 – 3½" squares
  - 1 – fabric #3 – 3½" square
  - 4 – fabric #1/#4/5# quad-triangle units
- Carefully follow the placement of the pieced units as shown.
- Follow the arrows to press the seams.
- Make 4. The blocks should measure 9½" square (unfinished).
- Square up if necessary.

Step 6: Assemble the Bear Paw Block

- For the Bear Paw block use:
  - 1 – fabric #2 – 3½" square
  - 4 – fabric #6 – 3½" x 8" rectangles
  - 4 – fabric #3 – 5½" squares
  - 4 – fabric #1 – 2½" squares
  - 16 – fabric #1/#3 HSTs
- Carefully follow the placement of the pieced units as shown.
- Follow the arrows to press the seams.
- Make 4. The block should measure 18½" square (unfinished).
- Square up if necessary.

Step 7: Assemble the Quilt Top

- Follow the diagram and carefully rotate the blocks as needed to lay out the quilt top as shown.
- Sew the blocks into rows; sew the rows together.
- Add the inner border, piecing the strips as needed.
- Add the outer border, piecing the strips as needed.
- Optionally, insert Prairie Points in the border. (See the quilt photo on page 62.)
- Layer batting and backing, and baste. Quilt as desired and add binding.
- Sign the back of your quilt in permanent ink, or sign and add a label. ENJOY!

Quilt assembly

Pastel Version

Designed by the author;
made by Claire Neal, Hampton Roads, VA;
machine quilted by Carolyn Archer, Ohio Star Quilting

I changed the placement of the values in this pretty pastel version and positioned the center pieced motif on point to achieve a more dramatic look. The chain is no longer the focal point. The Bear Paw blocks take a more supporting role and recede into the background. The overall design is still lovely and I think this quilt really shines with the use of fabrics in the cooler tones.

Bonus Layout!

You would need 32 Glacier blocks, 16 Northern Lights blocks, and 16 Bear Paw blocks for this layout.

NORTH TO ALASKA, 50" x 50", designed and made by the author; quilted by Birgit Schüller, Riegelsberg, Germany, Creative BiTS
Resides in the private collection of Robert and Cheri Wallace.

North to Alaska

Quilt size: 52" x 52"

Finished block size: 9" x 9"

Skill level: Intermediate

This is another quilt I designed specifically to teach on a quilting cruise to Alaska. However, the design is so terrific I want to share it with you because I know you'll just love it! The blocks relate to Alaskan towns or images you'd readily see in that great forty-ninth state. Of course the blocks aren't really difficult to piece but when they are combined, they become extraordinary! The thing you need to know, though, is to carefully choose fabrics #3, #4, #5, and #6 so they are medium in value; they should all look beautifully coordinated when laid together side by side.

Whether you ever plan to go to Alaska or you've traveled there many times, you'll want to make this beautiful quilt for your favorite outdoorsman or the nature-lover in you!

Fabric Requirements and Cutting Instructions

- Cut all strips across the WOF (selvage to selvage).
- You may choose to use the TRI RECs tools or the templates provided (page 93).

FABRIC	YARDS	INSTRUCTIONS
Fabric #1 Lightest Background	1¾ yards	• Cut (2) 3½" strips; subcut (24) 3½" x 3½" squares. • Cut (1) 2" strip. *[Step 1b]* • Cut (2) 3½" strips. *[Step 1a]* • Cut (9) 3½" strips for HSTs. *[Step 2]* • Cut (2) 3½" strips for use with TRI tool or template provided. *[Step 4a]*
Fabric #2 Medium light	¾ yard	• Cut (1) 2" strip. *[Step 1b]* • Cut (1) 2" strip; cut (8) 2" squares. *[Step 1c]* • Cut (2) 3½" strips. *[Step 1a]* • Cut (3) 3½" strips for HSTs. *[Step 2a]*
Fabric #3 Medium	½ yard	• Cut (1) 2" strips; cut (2) 2" squares. *[Step 1c]* • Cut (1) 7" strip; subcut (1) 6⅞" square. Cut square 1x diagonally to yield 2 triangles. *[Step 3]* • Cut remaining 7" strip in half lengthwise to yield (2) 3½" strips for HSTs. *[Step 2c]* • Cut (1) 3½" strip for use with RECS tool. *[Step 4b]*

(continued)

(continued)

FABRIC	YARDS	INSTRUCTIONS
Fabric #4 Medium	½ yard	• Cut (1) 2" strips; cut (2) 2" squares. *[Step 1c]* • Cut (1) 7" strip; subcut (1) 6⅞" square. Cut square in half once diagonally to yield 2 triangles. *[Step 3]* • Cut remaining 7" strip in half lengthwise to yield (2) 3½" strips for HSTs. *[Step 2c]* • Cut (1) 3½" strip for use with RECS tool. *[Step 4b]*
Fabric #5 Medium	⅓ yard	• Cut (1) 2" strips; cut (2) 2" squares. *[Step 1c]* • Cut (1) 7" strip; subcut (1) 6⅞" square. Cut square in half once diagonally to yield 2 triangles. *[Step 3]* • Cut the remaining 7" strip in half lengthwise to yield (2) 3½" strips for HSTs. *[Step 2c]* • Cut (1) 3½" strip for use with RECS tool. *[Step 4b]*
Fabric #6 Medium	½ yard	• Cut (1) 2" strips; cut (2) 2" squares. *[Step 1c]* • Cut (1) 7" strip; subcut (1) 6⅞" square. Cut square in half once diagonally to yield 2 triangles. *[Step 3]* • Cut remaining 7" strip in half lengthwise to yield (2) 3½" strips for HSTs. *[Step 2c]* • Cut (1) 3½" strip for use with RECS tool. *[Step 4b]*
Fabric #7 Multicolor Medium dark	1¼ yards	• Cut (5) 5½" strips for the outer border. • Cut (1) 6⅞" strip; subcut (2) 6⅞" squares. Cut squares 1x diagonally to yield 4 triangles. *[Step 3]* • Cut (2) 3½" strips. *[Step 2b]*
Backing	3½ yards	• 2 panels 30" x 60"
Batting		• 60" x 60"
Binding	½ yard	• Cut (6) 2¼" strips. Join end-to-end.

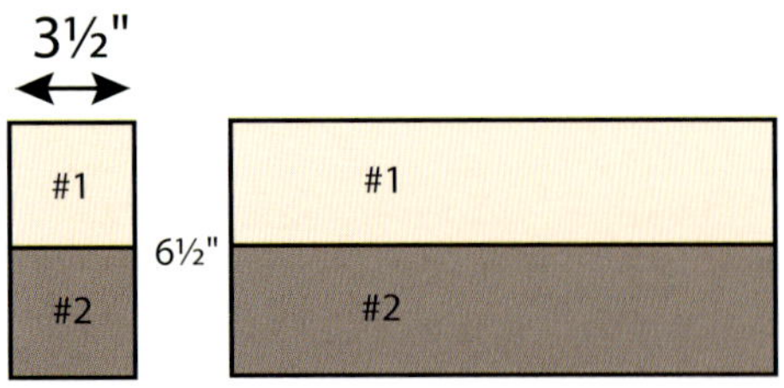

Cut 16. *Make 2.*

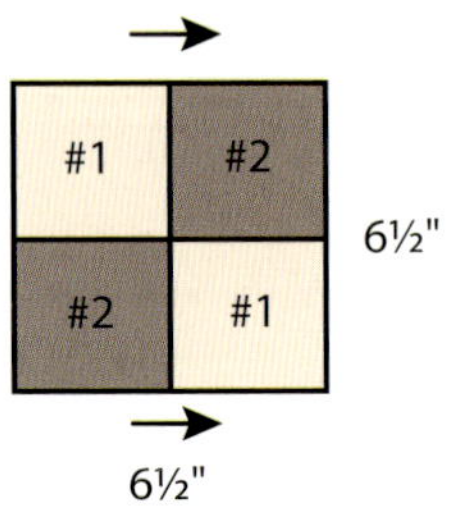

Make 8.

Step 1: Construct the Four-Patch Units

Step 1a

- Make 2 strip-sets with fabric #1 and fabric #2 – 3½" strips as shown. Press the seam closed first, then press the seam toward fabric #2.
- Cut 16 – 3½" segments.
- Join 2 segments to make a four-patch unit as shown. Press the unit closed, then press seam to one side.
- Make 8. The four-patch units should measure 6½" square (unfinished).
- Square up if necessary.

Step 1b

- Make 2 strip-sets using fabric #1 and fabric #2 – 2" strips.
- Cut 16 – 2" segments.
- Join 2 segments to make a four-patch unit as shown. Press the unit closed, then press seam to one side.
- Make 8. The four-patch units should measure 3½" square (unfinished).
- Square up if necessary.

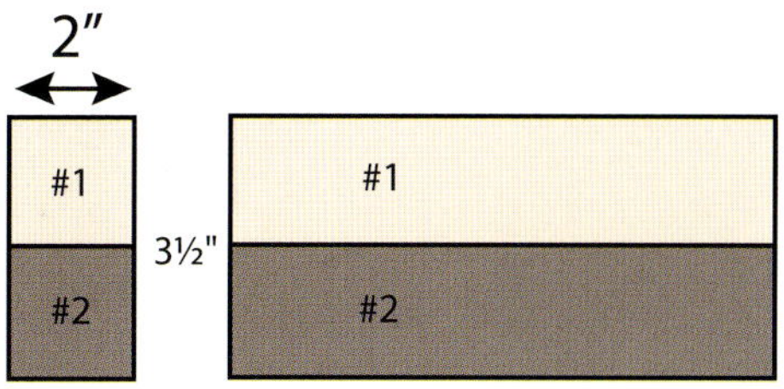

Cut 16. Make 2.

Step 1c

- Using 8 fabric #2 – 2" squares, and 2" squares of fabrics #3, #4, #5, and #6, make 1 EACH of the four-patch units in the combinations as shown.
- Press the seams away from fabric #2.
- The four-patch units should measure 3½" square (unfinished).
- Square up if necessary.

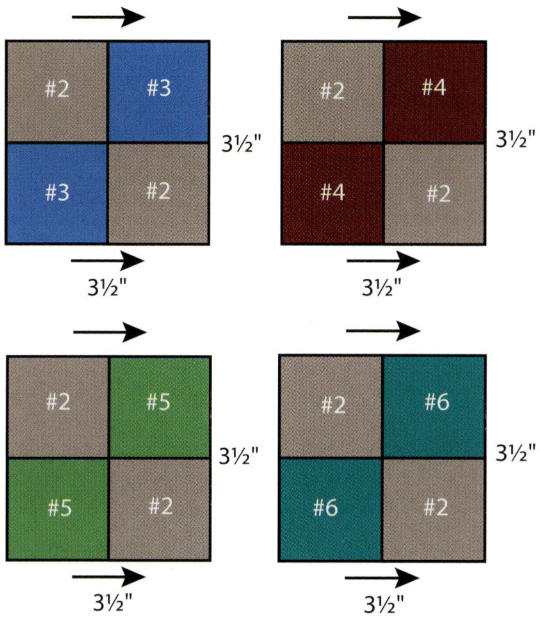

Make 1 each.

Step 2: Construct the Small HSTs

Step 2a

- Press a fabric #1 and fabric #2 – 3½" strip RST. Repeat to make 3 pairs of strips. *DO NOT SEW!*
- Use **Side B** of the ***EZ Flying Geese Ruler*** to cut 48 PAIRS of Side B triangles.
- Sew the #1/#2 B triangles to make 48 HSTs. Press the units closed, then press the seams toward fabric #2.
- The HSTs should measure 3½" square (unfinished). Trim the dog ears.
- Square up if necessary.

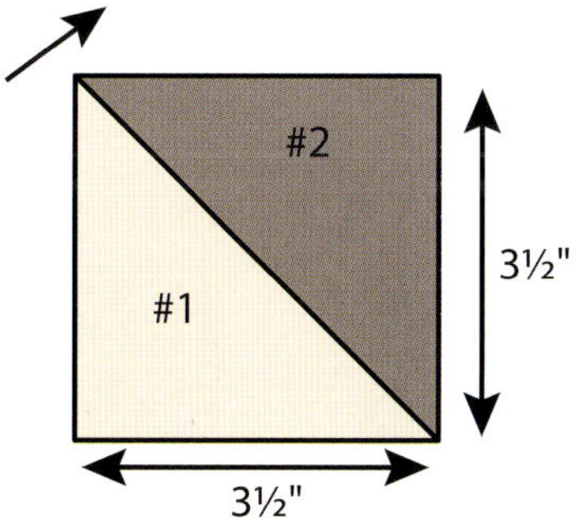

Make 48.

Step 2b

- Using same construction method as above, make a strip pair using fabric #1 and #7 – 3½" strips.
- Use **Side B** of the ***EZ Flying Geese Ruler*** to cut 8 B triangle PAIRS.
- Sew the #1/#7 B triangle pairs to make 8 HSTs. Press the units closed, then press the seams toward fabric #7.
- The HSTs should measure 3½" square (unfinished). Trim the dog ears.
- Square up if necessary.

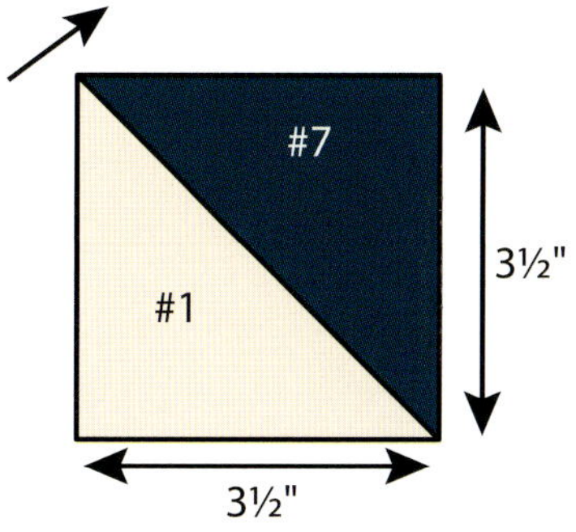

Make 8.

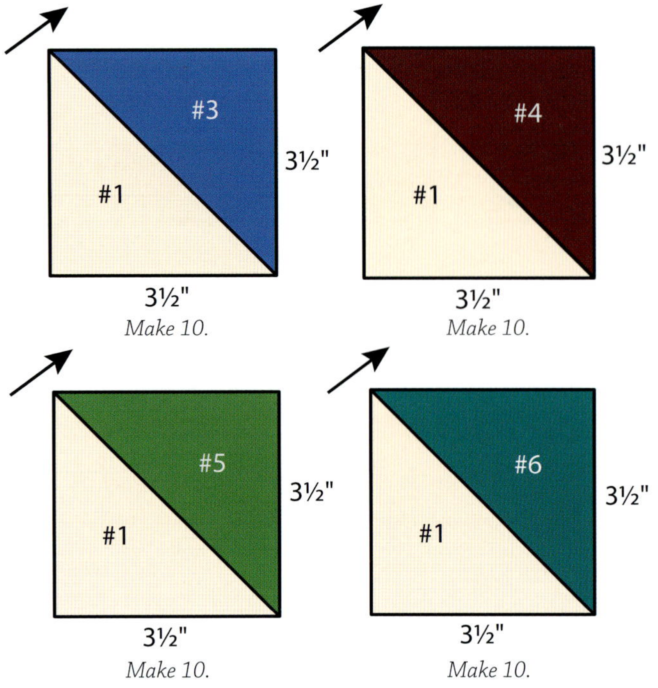

Step 2c

- Using same construction method as above, make strip pairs by combining 1 (of 4) fabric #1 – 3½" strip paired with 1 – 3½" strip each of fabrics #3, #4, #5, and #6.
- Use **Side B** of the ***EZ Flying Geese Ruler*** to cut 10 B triangle PAIRS from each strip pair.
- Sew the 10 B triangle pairs in the combinations shown to make a total of 40 HSTs. Press the units closed, then press the seams away from fabric #1.
- The HSTs should measure 3½" square (unfinished). Trim the dog ears.
- Square up if necessary.

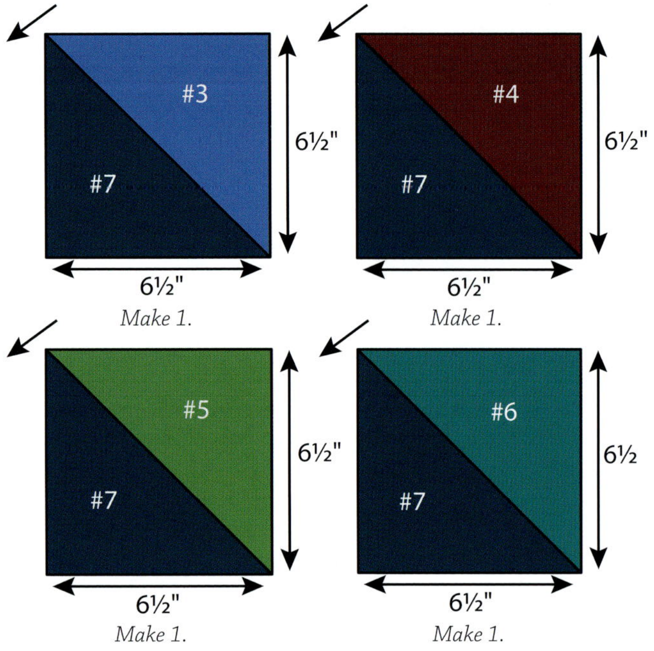

Step 3: Construct the Large HSTs

- Combine triangles cut from fabric #7 – 6⅞" squares with triangles from 6⅞" squares from fabrics #3, #4, #5, and #6 to yield 1 HST each.
- Press the units closed, then press the seams toward fabric #7.
- The HSTs should measure 6½" square (unfinished). Trim the dog ears.
- Square up if necessary.

Step 4: Construct the Star Points

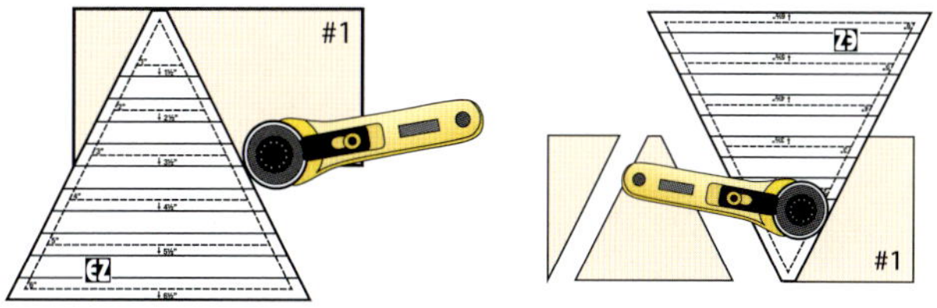

Step 4a

- Fold a fabric #1 - 3½" strip of fabric in half RST and use the TRI tool or the template (page 93) to cut 16 TRI units as shown.

Step 4b

- Use the RECS tool or the template (page 93) with (1) 3½" strip EACH of fabrics #3, #4, #5, and #6. Fold each strip RST! You need mirror image units!
- Cut 4 pairs of RECS units from each fabric strip as shown. Make sure to trim the nipped corners using the RECS tool as a guide.

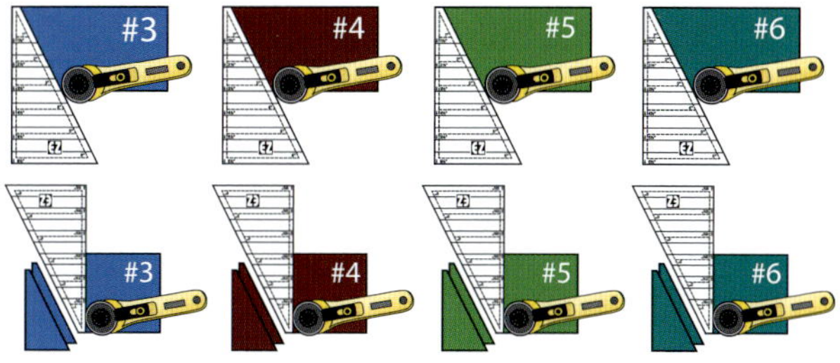

Make 4 pair. *Make 4 pair.* *Make 4 pair.* *Make 4 pair.*

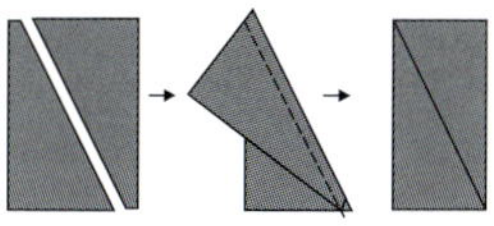

#3,#4,#5,#6

Step 4c

- Sew fabric #1 TRI units to the fabric #3, #4, #5, and #6 RECS units to make the Star points.
- The units should measure 3½" square (unfinished). Trim the dog ears.
- Square up if necessary.

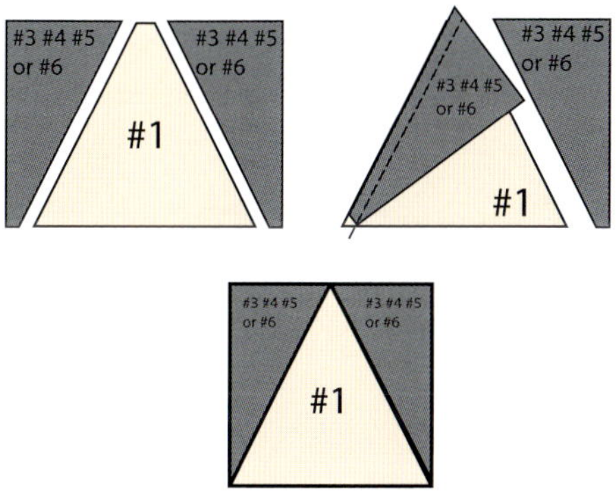

Step 5a: Assemble the Northern Lights Blocks

- Make each Northern Lights block using:
    - 1 fabric #1/#2 – 6½" four-patch unit
    - 4 – 3½" fabric #1/#2 HSTs
    - 1 – 3½" fabric #1#7 HSTs
- Press the seams in the direction of the arrows.
- Make 8 blocks.
- The blocks should measure 9½" square (unfinished).
- Square up if necessary.

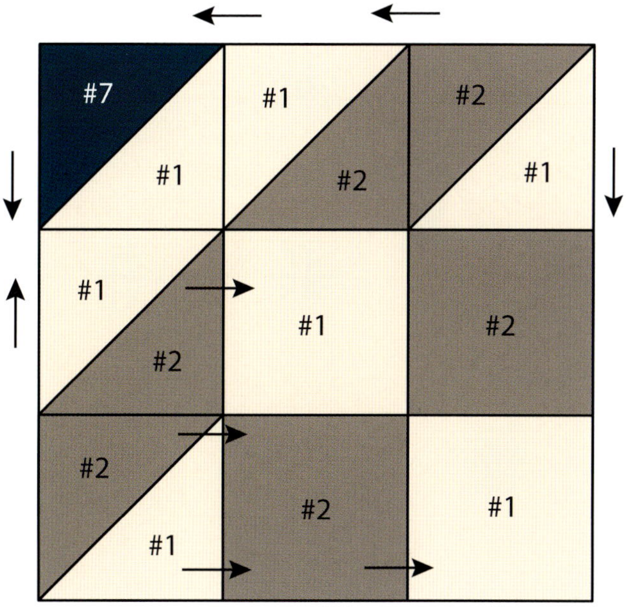

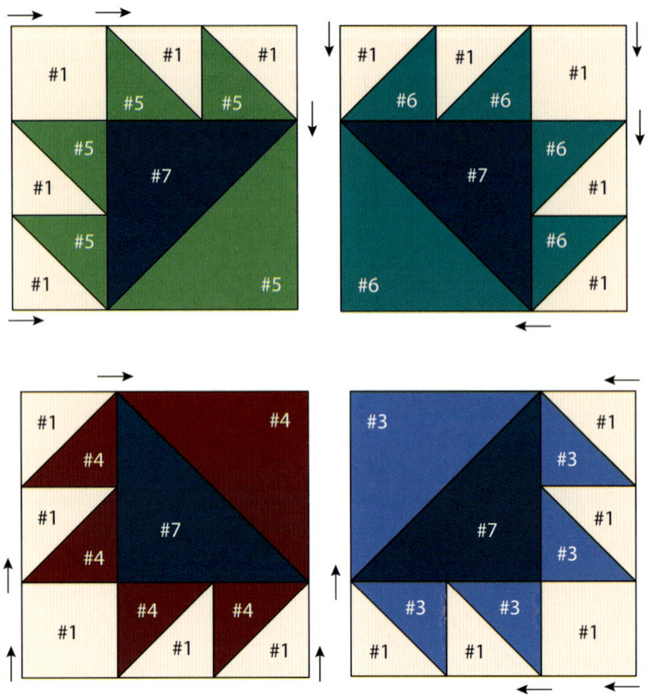

Step 5b: Assemble the Bear Paw Blocks

- Make each Bear Paw block using:
  - 1 fabric #1 – 3½" square
  - 1 – 6½" HST and 4 matching 3½" HSTs—one block EACH with fabrics #1, #3, #5, and #6
- Press the seams in the direction of the arrows.
- Make 4 blocks.
- The blocks should measure 9½" square (unfinished). Square up if necessary.

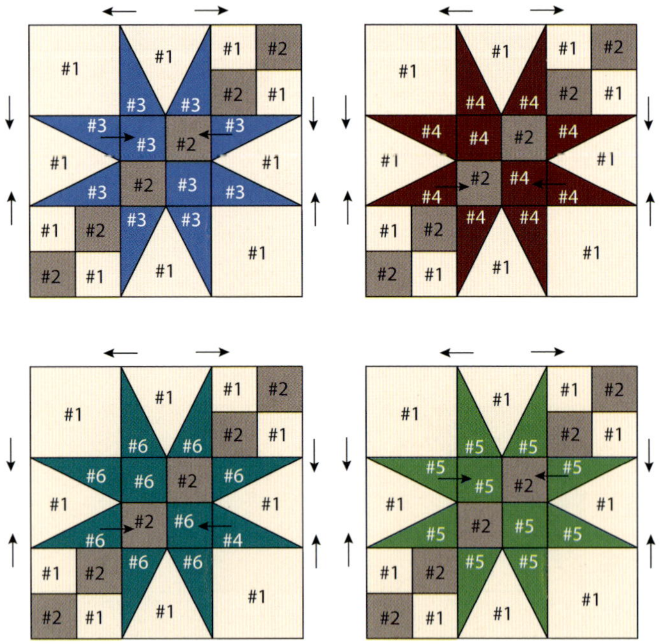

Step 5c: Assemble the Northern Star Blocks

- Make each Northern Star block using:
  - 2 fabric #1 – 3½" squares
  - 1 – 3½" four patch unit of fabrics #2/#3, #2/#4, #2/#5, or #2/#6
  - 2 – 3½" four patch units with fabrics #1/#2
  - 4 – 3½" TRI RECS units with fabrics #1/#3, #1/#4, #1/#5, or #1/#6
- Follow the arrows in the diagram to press the seams.
- Make 4 blocks.
- The blocks should measure 9½" square (unfinished). Square up if necessary.

Step 6: Assemble the Quilt Top

- Lay out the blocks as shown.
- Sew the blocks into rows.
- Sew the rows together.
- Piece the inner border as shown using the remaining HSTs and 3½" fabric #1 squares as shown. Add to the sides and top and bottom of the quilt top.
-

Step 7

- Add the outer border strips to complete the quilt top.
- Layer the quilt top, batting, and backing; baste and quilt as desired.

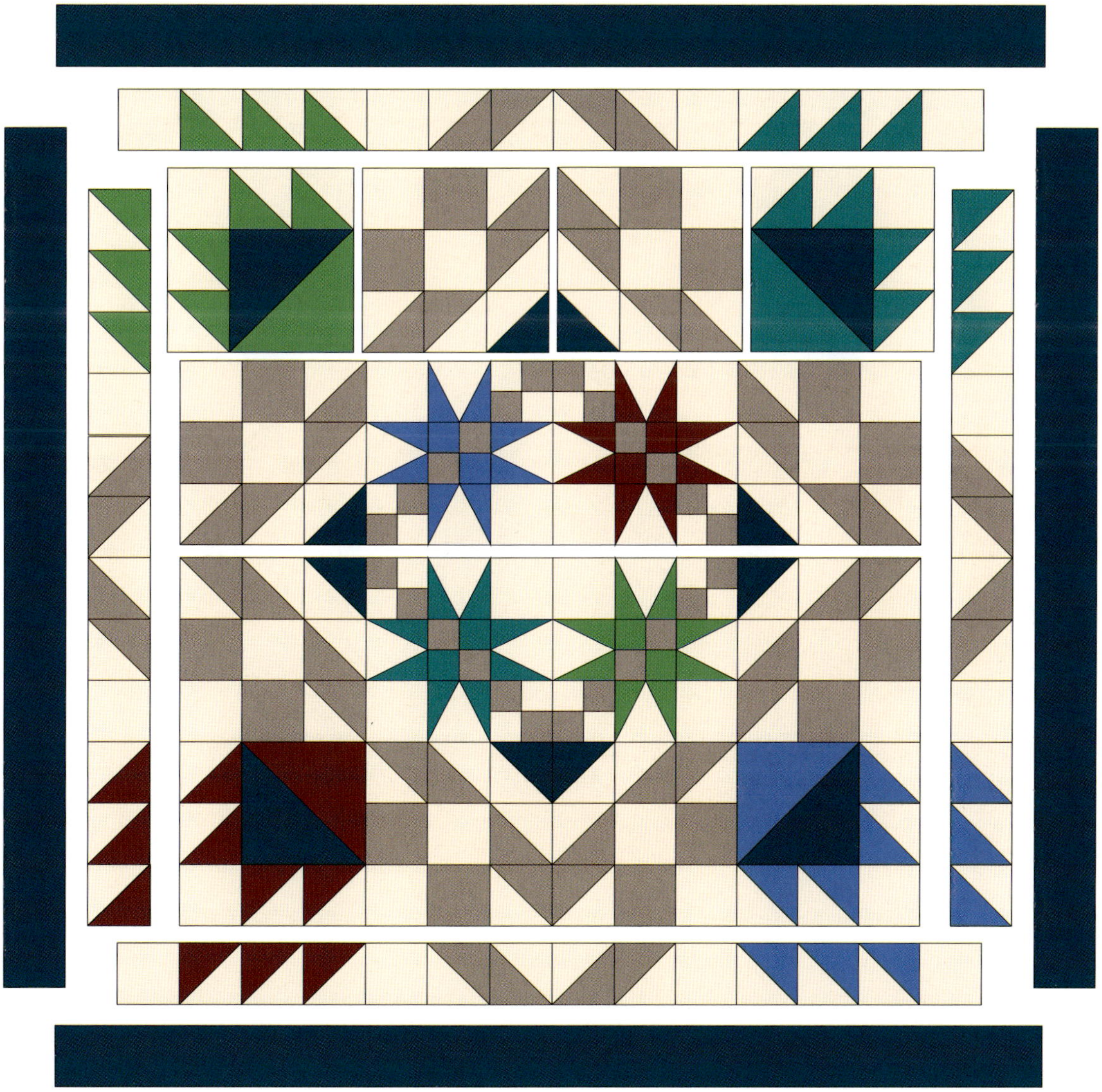

Quilt assembly

GINGER AND TEA LEAVES, 68" x 68", designed and made by the author; quilted by Carolyn Archer, Ohio Star Quilting

Ginger and Tea Leaves

Quilt size: 68" x 68"

Finished block size: 9" x 9"

Skill level: Skilled Beginner

Two pretty blocks: A Ginger Jar block and a Tea Leaf block. Pretty fabrics with hints of ginger and oriental blossoms plus a striking navy blue accent fabric are the perfect combination for a taste of the orient. Both blocks are constructed using basic quilting units but put them side by side and the secondary design makes them truly extraordinary! This quilt whips up quite quickly, and you'll love choosing a favorite focus fabric to really shine!

Fabric Requirements and Cutting Instructions

• Cut all strips WOF (selvage to selvage).

FABRIC	YARDS	INSTRUCTIONS
Fabric #1 Main Print Multicolor	1 yard	• Cut (6) 5½" strips for the outer border. *[Step 3]*
Fabric #2 Light Background	1¾ yards	• Cut (10) 3⅞" strips; subcut (92) 3⅞" x 3⅞" squares. Cut the squares 1x diagonally to yield 184 triangles *[Steps 1a, 1b, and 2a]*. • Cut (2) 3½" strips; subcut (16) 3½" x 3½" squares. *[Step 2d]* • Cut (1) 4¼" strip; subcut (8) 4¼" x 4¼" squares. Cut squares 2x diagonally to yield 32 triangles. *[Step 2b]* • Cut (2) 3⅜" strips; subcut (16) 3⅜" x 3⅜" squares. Cut squares 1x diagonally to yield 32 triangles. *[Step 2c]*
Fabric #3 Medium Gold	½ yard	• Cut (2) 7" strips; subcut (10) 7" x 7" squares. Cut the squares 1x diagonally to yield 20 triangles. *[Step 1b]*
Fabric #4 Medium Red	⅝ yard	• Cut (2) 3½" strips; subcut (16) 3½" x 3½" squares. *[Step 2d]* • Cut (2) 3⅞" strips; subcut (16) 3⅞" x 3⅞" squares. Cut the squares 1x diagonally to yield 32 triangles. *[Step 2b]* • Cut (1) 4¼" strip; subcut (8) 4¼" x 4¼" squares. Cut the squares 2x diagonally to yield 32 triangles. *[Step 2b]*

(continued)

(continued)

FABRIC	YARDS	INSTRUCTIONS
Fabric #5 Medium Apricot	½ yard	• Cut (2) 7" strips; subcut (10) 7" x 7" squares. Cut the squares 1x diagonally to yield 20 triangles. *[Step 1b]*
Fabric #6 Dark Dark red	½ yard	• Cut (4) 3⅞" strips; subcut (32) 3⅞" x 3⅞" squares. Cut the squares 1x diagonally to yield 64 triangles. *[Step 2a]*
Fabric #7 Dark Navy blue	1¼ yards	• Cut (2) 3½" strips; subcut (20) 3½" x 3½" squares. *[Step 1b]* • Cut (2) 3⅞" strips; subcut (20) 3⅞" x 3⅞" squares. Cut the squares 1x diagonally to yield 40 triangles. *[Step 1a]* • Cut (1) 5½" strip; subcut (4) 5½" x 5½" squares. *[Step 3]* • Cut (6) 2½" strips; for the inner border. Piece as needed. *[Step 3]*
Fabric #8 Dark Dark gold	¼ yard	• Cut (1) 5½" strip; subcut (16) 5½" x 5½" rectangles.
Backing	4¼ yards	• 2 panels 40" x 77"
Batting		• 76" x 76"
Binding	¾ yard	• Cut (8) 2¼" strips; join end-to-end.

Make 40.

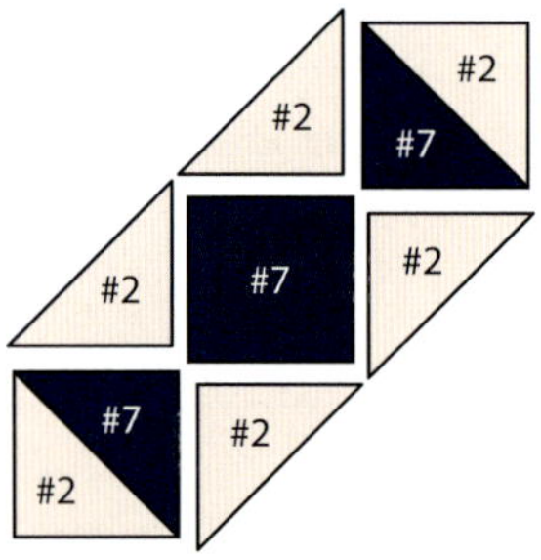

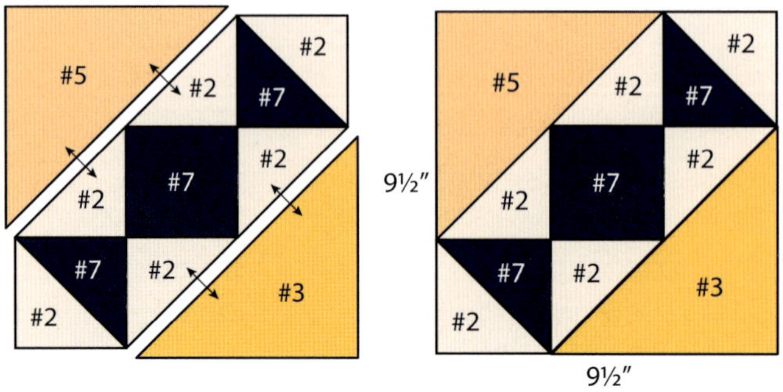

Make 20.

Step 1: Ginger Jar Block

Step 1a: Assembling the HSTs

- Sew fabric #2 and #7 B triangles cut from the 3⅞" squares RST to make 40 HSTs as shown.
- Press the seams toward the darker fabric. The HSTs should meausure 3½" square (unfinished).
- Join fabric #7 3½" squares, fabric #2 triangles, and the HSTs as shown. Repeat to make a total of 20 units.

Step 1a: Assembling the HSTs

- Add fabric #3 and #5 triangles cut from 7" squares to the pieced units.

  NOTE: These triangles are slightly oversized.
- Press the seams toward the large triangles.
- Trim the blocks to measure 9½" square (unfinished).

Step 2: Tea Leaf Block

Step 2a: Assembling the HSTs

- Sew fabric #2 and #6 triangles cut from the 3⅞" squares RST to make 64 HSTs as shown.
- Press the seams toward the darker fabric. The HSTs should measure 3½" square (unfinished).

Step 2b: Assembling the Triple-Triangle Units

- Sew fabric #2 and #4 triangles cut from 4¼" squares to make double-triangle units as shown.
- Add fabric #4 triangles cut from 3⅞" squares to create the triple-triangle units.
- Press the seams toward the larger triangles. The units should measure 3½" square (unfinished).
- Square up if necessary.

Step 2c: Assembling the Leaf Stems

- Sew a fabric #8 5½" x 2½" strip between 2 fabric #2 triangles.
- Press the seams toward the stem.
- Trim the ends off the stem to make 3½" square leaf stem units as shown. Make 16.

Step 2d: Assembling the Tea Leaf Block

- For each block, use:
  - 4 fabric #2/#6 HSTs
  - 2 triple-triangle units
  - 1 fabric #4 3½" square
  - 1 fabric #2 3½" square
  - 1 stem unit
- Press as shown by the arrows.
- Make 16. The blocks should measure 9½" square (unfinished). Square up if necessary.

Make 64.

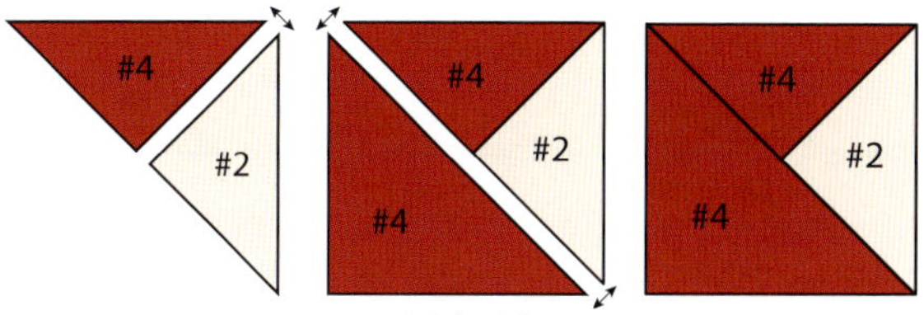

Make 32.

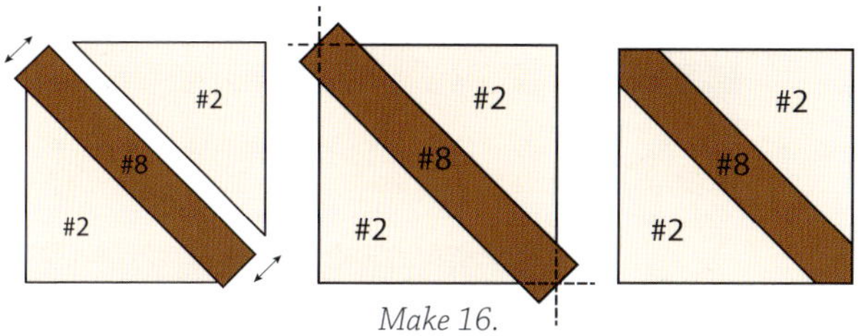

Make 16.

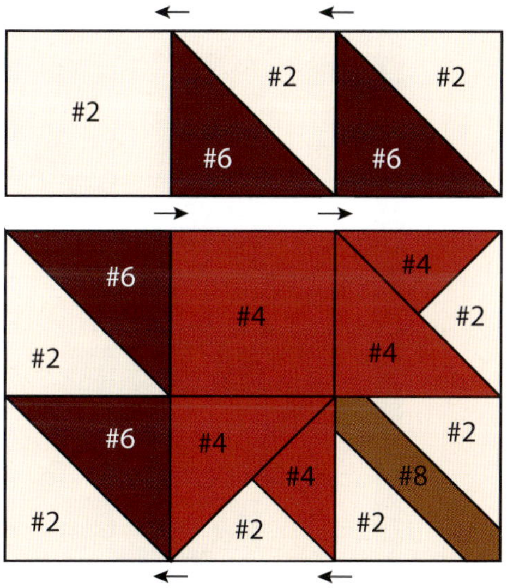

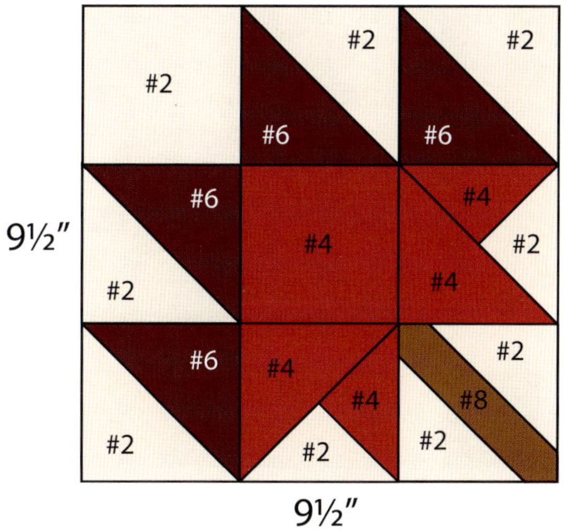

Make 16.

Step 3: Construct the Quilt Top

- Lay out the blocks as shown, paying careful attention to the orientation of the blocks, rotating them as needed to complete quilt top as shown.
- Sew the blocks into rows; sew the rows together.
- Add the inner borders. Press the seams away from the quilt center.
- Add the outer borders with 4 fabric #7 – 5½" squares in the corners. Press the seams away from the quilt center.
- Quilt, bind, and add a label. Enjoy!

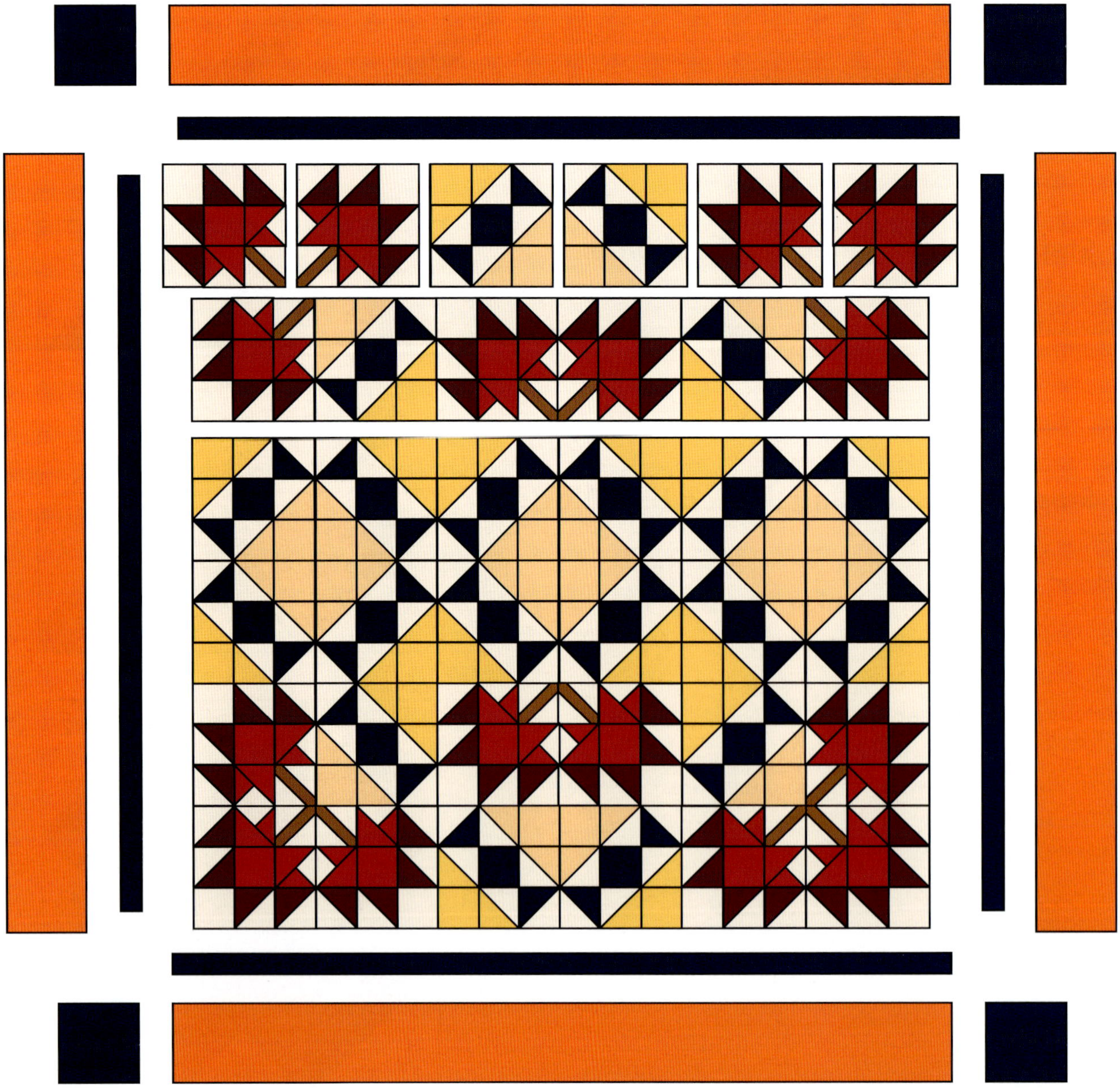

Quilt assembly

Pinwheel Twist, 54" x 54", designed and made by the author; quilted by Carolyn Archer, Ohio Star Quilting
You can choose to use a striped border fabric with mitered corners, as shown here, or select a multicolor print for the borders, as called for in the instructions.

Pinwheel Twist

Quilt size: 54" x 54"

Finished block size: 10" x 10"

Skill level: Skilled Beginner

Ready to do the twist? This is a stunning quilt that looks incredibly complex but is actually quite manageable if you take your time, step by step. Don't rush through the construction process. Once you master the piecing for the double-rectangle units, you'll find that adding them to your blocks opens a door to a whole new set of gorgeous design options. These nifty tools make the rotary cutting and piecing process oh-so-easy! So let's jump right in and do the Pinwheel Twist.

Fabric Requirements and Cutting Instructions

• Cut all strips across the WOF (selvage to selvage).

FABRIC	YARDS	INSTRUCTIONS
Fabric #1 Multicolor print	1¼ yards	• Cut (6) 5½" strips from LOF; and set aside for the outer border. *[Step 9]* • Cut (2) 5½" strips; subcut (8) 5½" x 5½" squares. *[Step 7]*
Fabric #2 Light Background	1¼ yards	• Cut (4) 3" strips; subcut (4) 3" x 3" squares. *[Step 6]* • Use Side A of the ***EZ Flying Geese Ruler*** to cut 16 A triangles. (You'll use a bit more than 1 strip.) *[Step 3]* Set aside the remaining full and partial strips. *[Steps 1 & 2]* • Cut (3) 3¼" strips; subcut (16) 3¼" x 6⅛" rectangles. *[Step 5]* • Cut (2) 5½" strips; subcut (8) 5½" x 5½" squares. *[Step 4]*
Fabric #3 Medium light	¼ yard	• Cut (2) 3" strips. *[Steps 2 & 3]*
Fabric #4 Medium	¾ yard	• Cut (1) 3" strip. *[Steps 2 & 3]* • Cut (5) 2½" strips; set aside for inner border. *[Step 9]*
Fabric #5 Medium dark	½ yard	• Cut (3) 3" strips; subcut (8) 3" x 3" squares. *[Step 4]* • Set aside the remaining 2 strips. *[Steps 1 & 2]*

(continued)

(continued)

FABRIC	YARDS	INSTRUCTIONS
Fabric #6 Dark	¾ yard	• Cut (3) 3" strip. *[Steps 2 & 5]* • Cut (2) 3" strips; subcut (16) 3" x 3" squares. *[Step 7]* • Cut (3) 3¼" strips; subcut (16) 3¼" x 6⅛" rectangles. *[Step 5]*
Backing	3½ yards	• 2 panels 30" x 60"
Batting		• 60" x 60"
Binding	½ yard	• Cut (6) 2¼" strips. Join end-to-end.

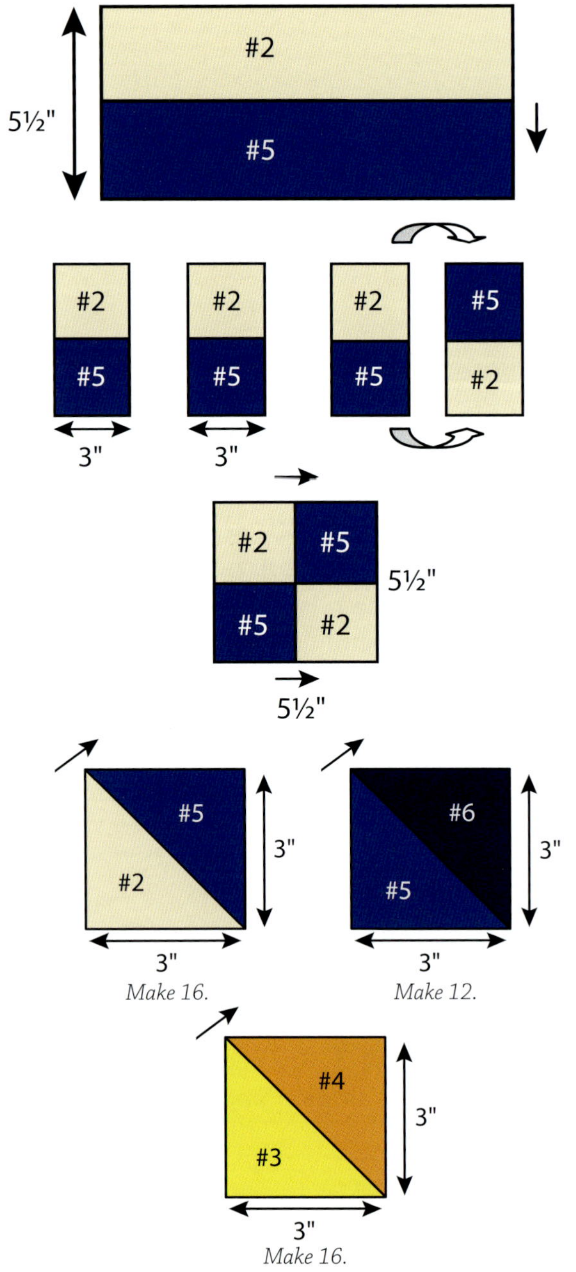

Step 1: Construct the Four-Patch Units

- Make a strip-set of fabric #2 and #5 – 3" strips. Press the seam closed then press the unit open with seam toward darker fabric.
- Cut 12 – 3" segments and rotate one unit and place RST on top of another unit.
- Sew 2 segments as shown to make a four-patch unit. Make 4. Set aside the remaining 4 two-patch segments for Step 6.
- Press each unit closed first, then open and press the seam to one side.
- The four-patch units should measure 5½" square unfinished. Square up if necessary.

Step 2: Construct the HSTs

- Place 3" fabric #2 and #5 strips RST.
- Use Side B of the EZ Flying Geese Ruler to cut 16 – 3" triangle B PAIRS. Refer to page 16 for directions to cut, sew, and trim the triangle units to make 16 HSTs. Press the seam allowance toward the darker fabric.
- Units should measure 3" x 3" unfinished. Square up if necessary.
- Repeat the process using 3" fabric #5 and #6 strips to make 12 HSTs.
- Repeat the process using 3" fabric #3 and #4 strips to make 16 HSTs.

Step 3: Construct the Flying Geese Units

- Refer to pages 16 & 17 for directions to make 16 flying geese units using:
    - 16 fabric #2 A triangles
    - 16 fabric #3 & #4 triangle B PAIRS
      NOTE: It is very important to layer fabric #3 on the bottom with fabric #4 on the top, RST!
- Add the B triangles as shown. Press the seams away from the center triangle.
- The flying geese units should measure 3" x 6" (unfinished). Square up if necessary.
- Make 16.

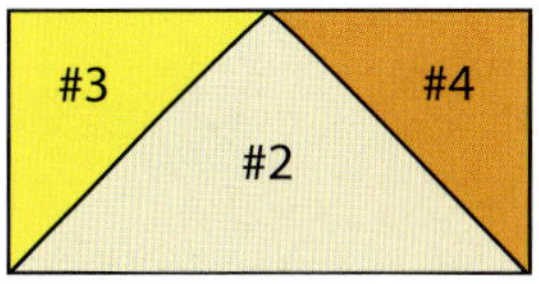

Make 16.

Step 4: Construct the Trimmed-Corner Squares

- Draw a diagonal line on the back of the fabric #5 – 3" squares.
- Place a 3" square RST on the corner of a fabric #2 – 5½" square and sew on the drawn line.
- Trim the corner ¼" from sewn line.
- Press the fabric #5 triangle open with seam away from the large, fabric #2 square.
- The unit should measure 5½" (unfinished).
- Square up if necessary.
- Make 8 units.

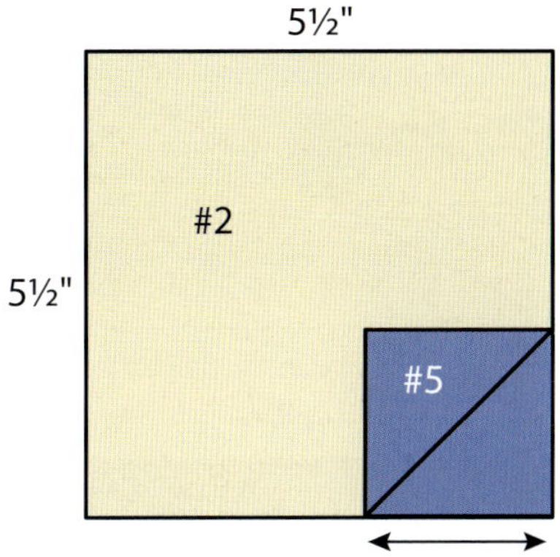

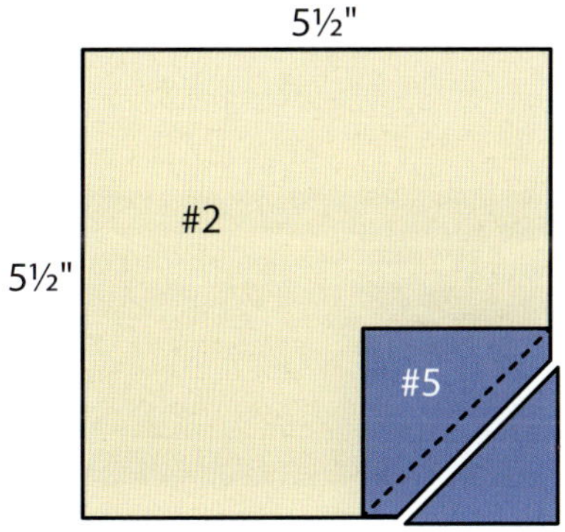

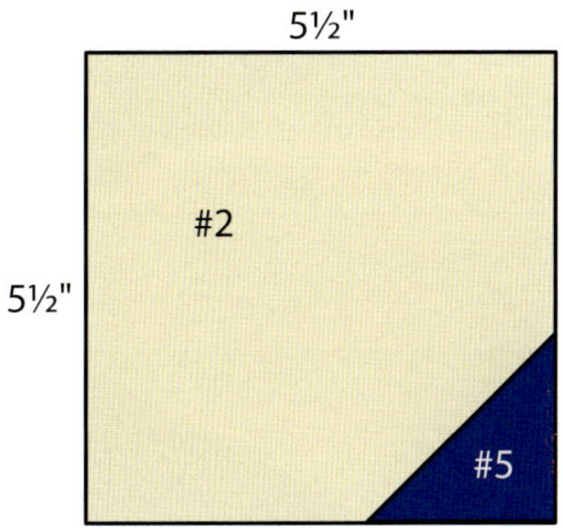

Make 8.

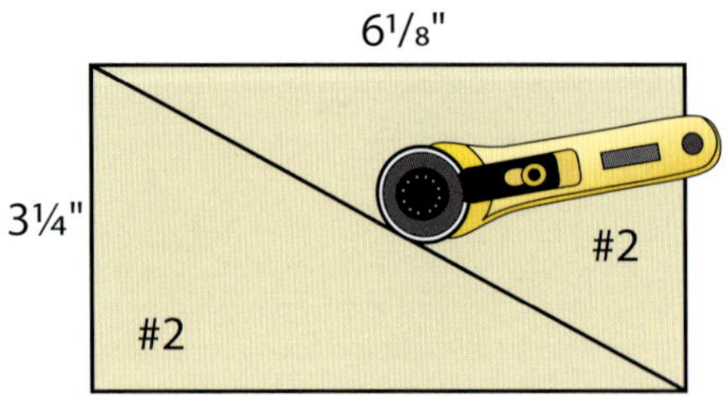

Cut 4 – fabric #2 rectangles.

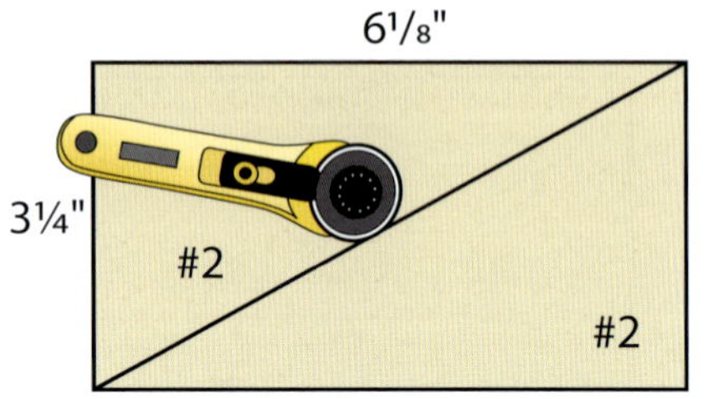

Cut 4 – fabric #2 rectangles.

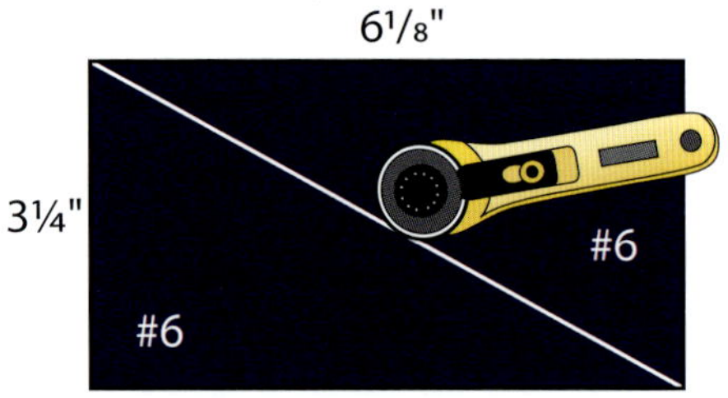

Cut 4 – fabric #6 rectangles.

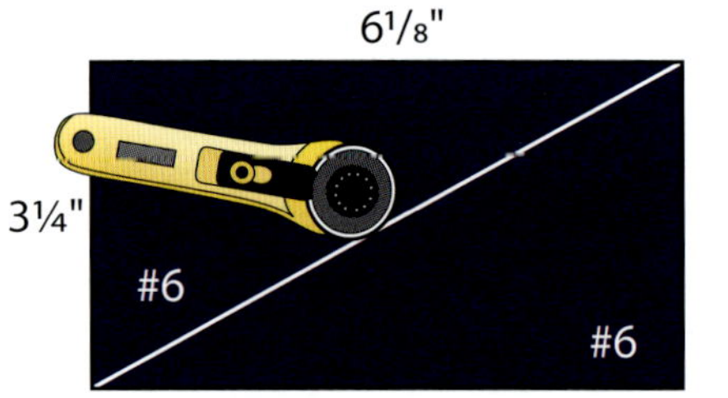

Cut 4 – fabric #6 rectangles.

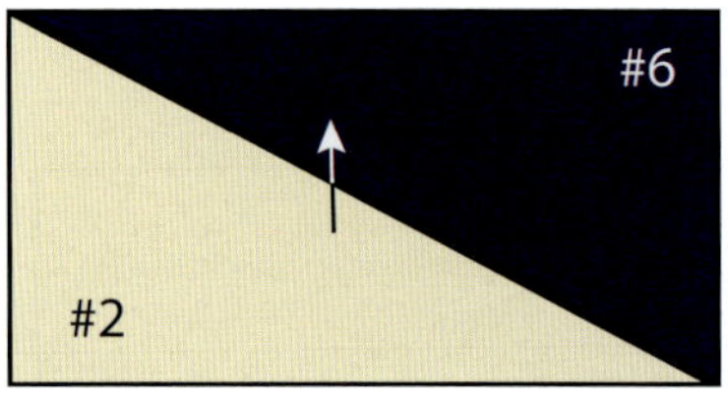

Make 16 half-rectangle units.

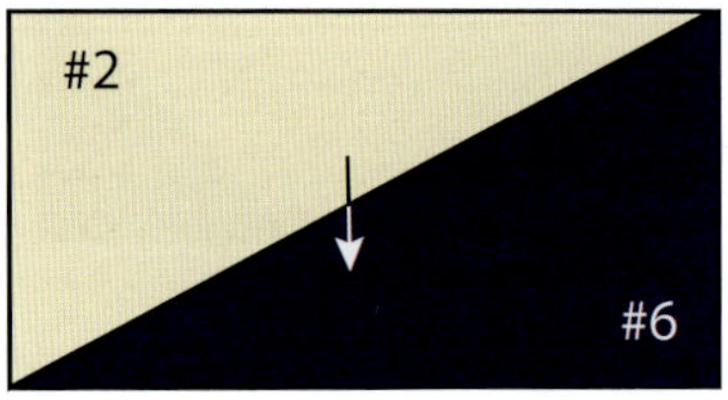

Make 16 half-rectangle units.

Step 5: Construct the Half-Rectangle Units

- Stack 4 fabric #2 – 3¼" x 6⅛" rectangles RSU.
- Cut the rectangles in half EXACTLY as shown (upper left corner to lower right corner) to yield 8 half-rectangles.

  NOTE: The direction and orientation of these cuts is extremely important.
- Stack the remaining 4 fabric #2 – 3¼" x 6⅛" rectangles RSU.
- Cut in half EXACTLY as shown (lower left corner to upper right corner) to yield 8 half-rectangles.
- Repeat the process with the 8 fabric #6 – 3¼" x 6⅛" rectangles, cutting 4 in one direction and 4 in the opposite direction.
- Make 16 half-rectangle units EXACTLY as shown.
- Make 16 half-rectangle units EXACTLY as shown.

Step 6: Construct the Chain Blocks

- Assemble each Chain block using:
  - 2 fabric #2/#5 trimmed-corner units
  - 1 fabric #2/#5 four-patch unit
  - 1 fabric #2/#5 two-patch segments
  - 1 fabric #5/#6 HST
- Press the seams as shown by the arrows.
- Make 4 blocks.
- The blocks should measure 10½" square (unfinished). Square up if necessary.

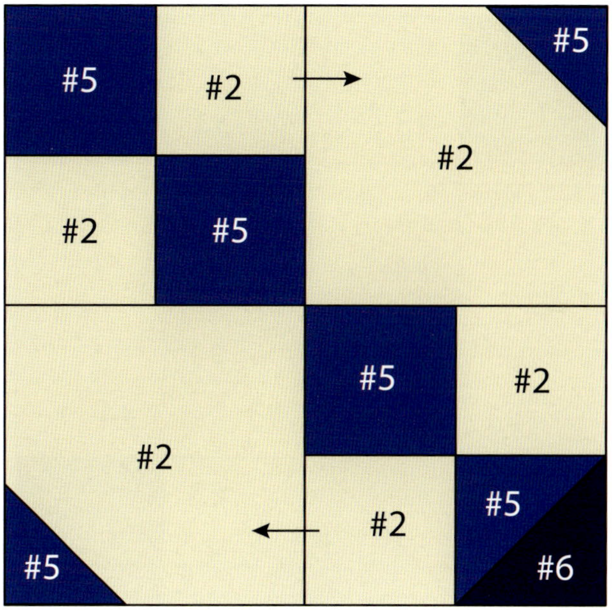

Make 4.

Step 7: Assemble the Twister Blocks

- Assemble each Twister block using:
  - 2 fabric #6 – 3" squares
  - 2 fabric #2/#5 HSTs
  - 1 fabric #1 – 5" square
  - 2 fabric #2/#6 half-rectangle units
  - 2 fabric #2/#6 mirror image half-rectangle units
- Press the seams as shown by the arrows.
- Make 8 blocks.
- The blocks should measure 10½" square (unfinished). Square up if necessary.

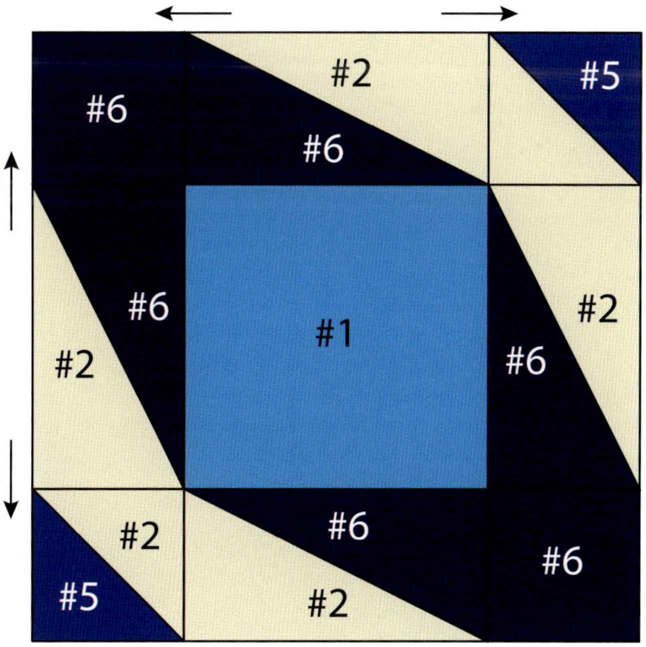

Make 8.

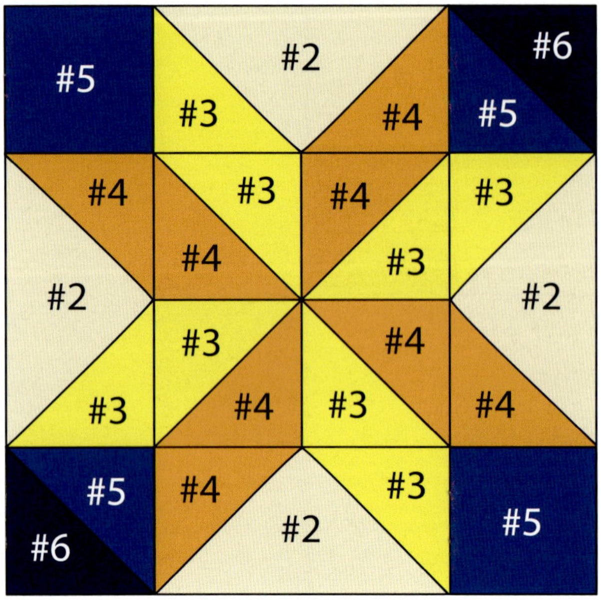

Make 4.

Step 8: Assemble the Cross Block

- Assemble each Cross block using:
    - 2 fabric #5 – 3" squares
    - 2 fabric #5/#6 HSTs
    - 4 fabric #3/#4 HSTs
    - 4 flying geese units
- Make 4 blocks.
- Press the seams as shown by the arrows.
- The blocks should measure 10½" square (unfinished). Square up if necessary.

Step 9: Assemble the Quilt Top

- Lay out the blocks in rows as shown, rotating the blocks as needed.
- Sew the blocks in rows: sew the rows together.
- Add the inner border.
- Add the outer border.
- Layer the quilt top, batting, and backing; baste and quilt as desired.

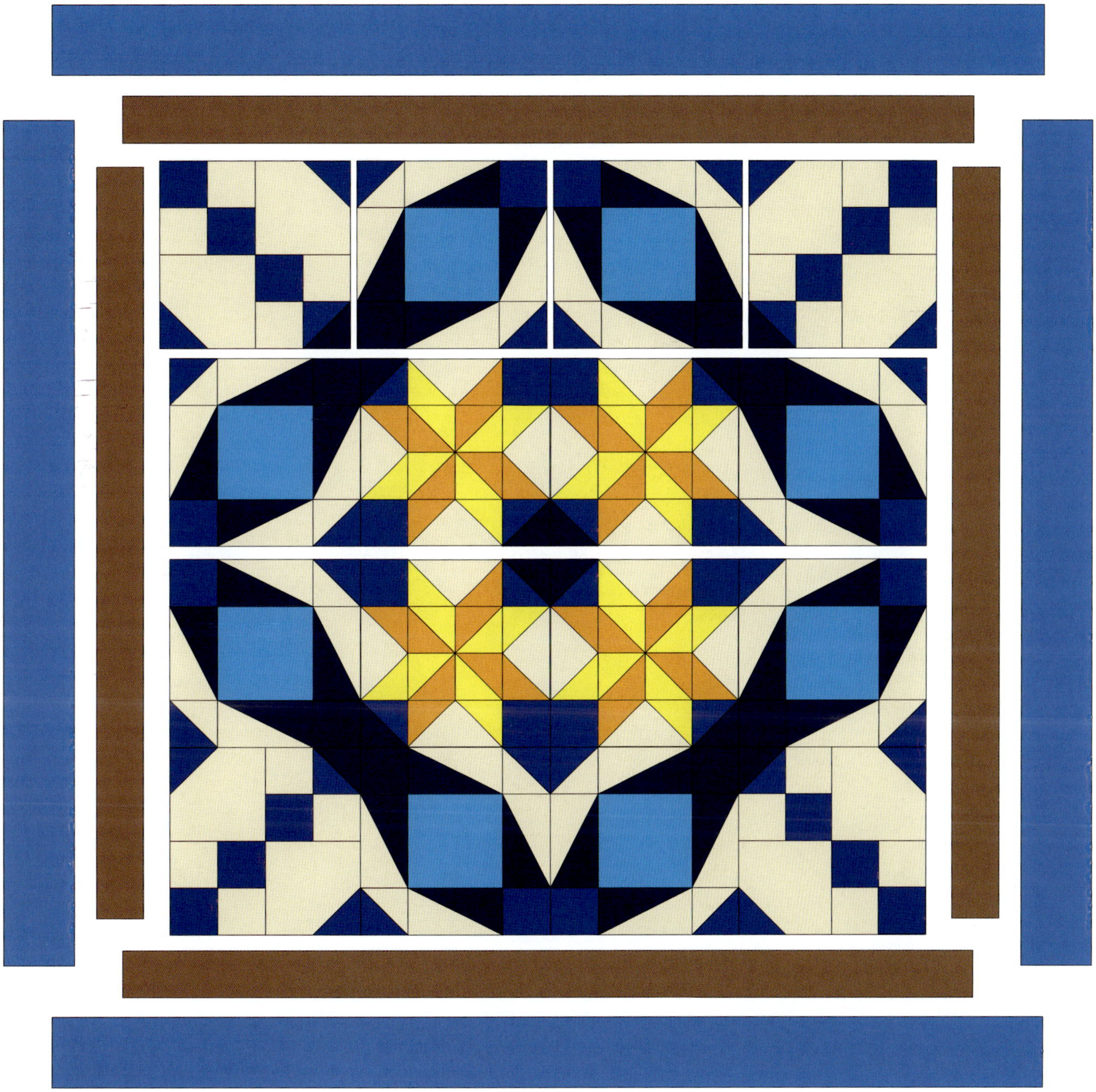

Quilt assembly

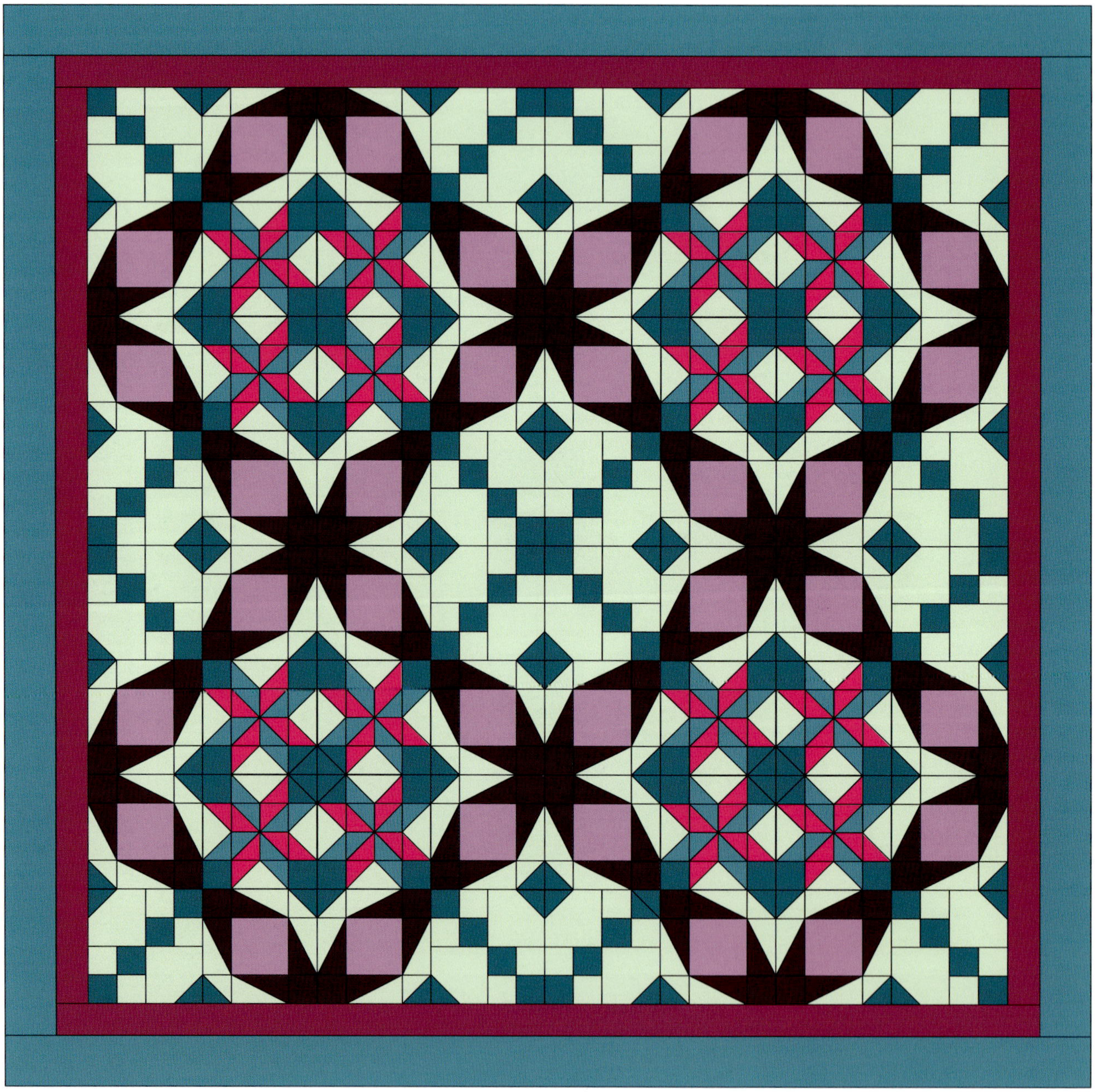

Bonus layout!
To make this lage size quilt you would simply need to add more blocks: 16 Chain blocks, 32 Twister blocks, and 16 Cross blocks.

Pinwheel Twist, 54" x 94"

Twin Version:

Designed by the author; made by Claire Neal, Hampton Roads, VA; quilted by Carolyn Archer, Ohio Star Quilting

This twin bed topper is the same quilt constructed using twice the number of blocks. The design looks terrific whether you use batiks, print fabrics, or, for a more modern look, solid fabrics.

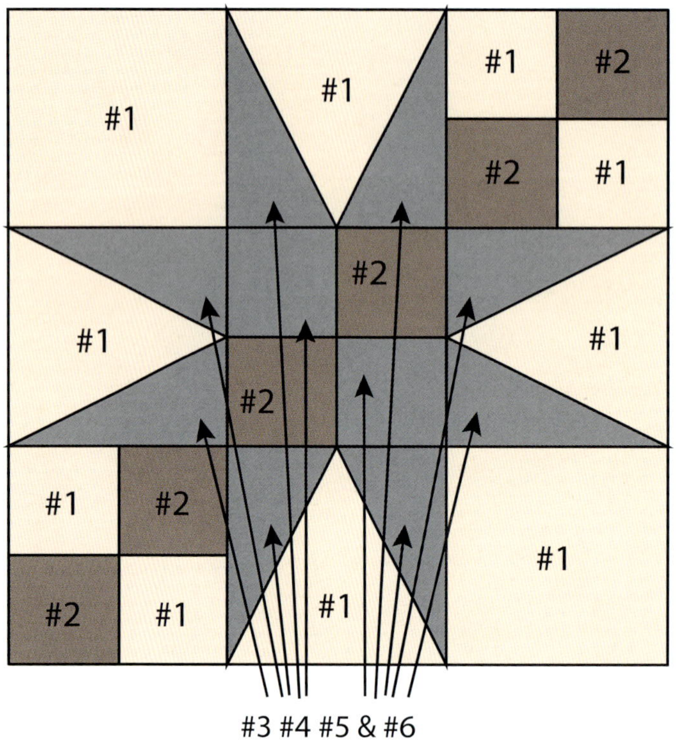

Northern Star Block

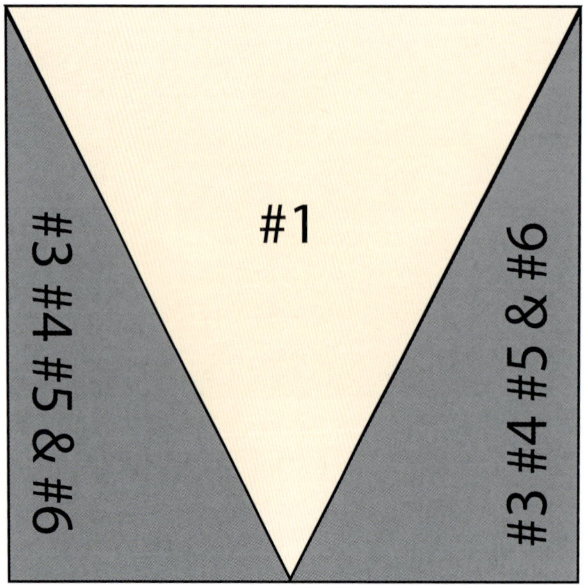

Star Points

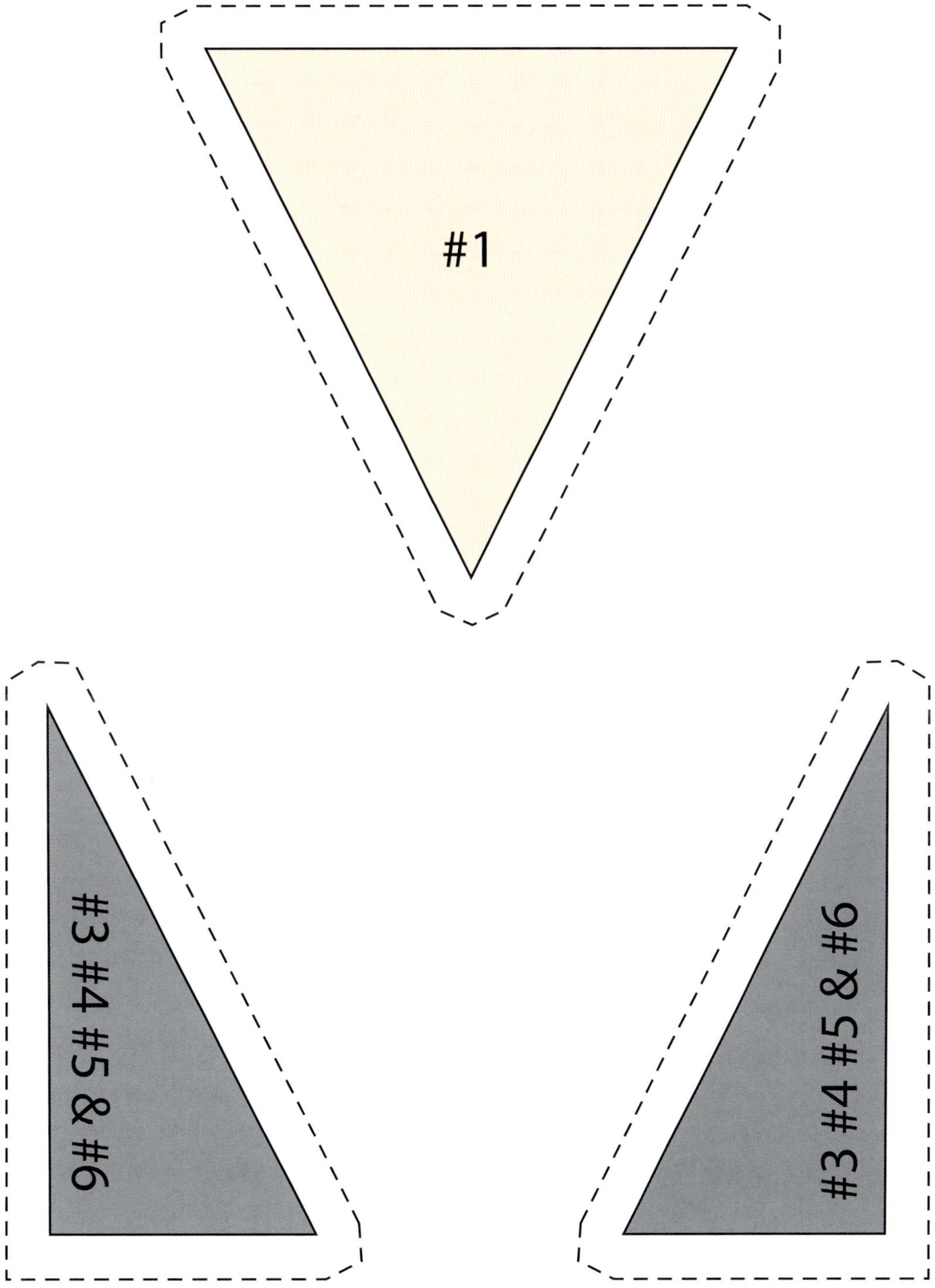
#1
#3 #4 #5 & #6
#3 #4 #5 & #6

Resource Guide

Contributors

It is with sincere and heartfelt appreciation I would like to thank the following companies and individuals for their support of products and services that have helped to make this book possible. The fabric, batting, tools, and supplies featured or mentioned in this book are listed because they are truly the products I love and rely on to create my own quilts. I'm frequently asked about my choice of products and I'm happy to list them here so you, too, can buy and use these top quality items to enhance your own quilting experience and results.

EZ Flying Geese Ruler

EZ Jelly Roll Ruler

both by Kimberly Einmo

TRI RECs Tool

by Darlene Zimmernan

You can order these tools directly from me at my website:
www.kimberlyeinmo.com
OR at: ***www.simplicity.com***

American Quilter's Society

P.O. Box 3290
Paducah, KY 42002-3290
Phone: 270-898-7903
www.americanquilter.com

Electric Quilt Company

419 Gould Street, Suite 2
Bowling Green, OH 43402-3047
Phone: 419-352-1134
www.electricquilt.com

Robert Kaufman Fabrics

129 West 132nd Street
Los Angeles, CA 90061
Phone: 800-877-2066
www.robertkaufman.com

Timeless Treasures Fabrics

483 Broadway, 4th Floor
New York, NY 10013
Phone: 212-226-1400
www.ttfabrics.com

Fairfield Processing Corp.

P.O. Box 1157
Danbury, CT 06813-1157
Phone: 800-980-8000
www.poly-fil.com

Aurifil

184 Shuman Blvd. Suite 200
Naperville, IL 60563
Phone: 312-212-3485
info@aurifilusa.com

Koala Cabinets / Tacony Corporation

1760 Gilsinn Lane
Fenton, MO 63026
Phone: 636-349-3000
www.sewingandcraftclub.com

Rowenta USA

2199 Eden Road
Milville, NJ 08332
Phone: 800-ROWENTA
www.rowentausa.com

Prym Consumer USA, Inc.

P.O. Box 253
Burlington, WA 98233
Phone: 360-707-2828
www.dritz.com/brands/omnigrid/index.php

Clover Needlecraft Inc.

13438 Alondra Blvd.
Cerritos, CA 90703
www.clover-usa.com

Schmetz

9960 NW 116 Way, Suite 3
Medley, FL 33178
www.schmetz.com

The Strip Stick

Robert and Anne Babb
Babb Enterprises
Phone: 409-656-3013
www.thestripstick.com

Jilily Studio Needle Arts

Appliqué glue
11626 Sunset Hills Dr.
Highland, UT 84003
Phone: 801-234-9884
www.jililystudio.com

Longarm Machine Quilting Sources

Birgit Schüller/Creative BiTS

Schachtstrasse5
662w Riegelsberg, Germany
Email: birgit.schueller@creativebits.biz
Web: www.creativebits.biz

Carolyn Archer/Ohio Star Quilting

2895 Wilmington Road
Lebanon, OH 45036
Phone: 513-933-9008
Email: carcher3@roadrunner.com

About the Author

Kimberly Einmo

Photo by Bonnie McCaffery

Kimberly Einmo is an author, award-winning quilter, designer, international instructor and quilt judge. She has written six best-selling books published by the American Quilter's Society including ***Modern Quilts & More***, ***Precut Bonanza***, ***Jelly Roll Quilt Magic***, ***Jelly Roll Quilts & More***, ***Quilt A Travel Souvenir***, and ***Clever Combo Quilts***.

Kimberly has hosted five very popular online courses with over 105,000 students from around the world on **CRAFTSY** including the **2015 Summer BOM**, **Magical Blocks: Out of the Box**, **Magical Jelly Roll Quilts**, **Chain of Stars Mystery Quilt**, and **Amazing Applique**. Kimberly also writes a monthly column featured in *American Quilter Magazine* entitled "Kimberly's Korner" and she has written dozens of articles which have appeared in numerous publications including *American Patchwork and Quilting Magazine*, *McCall's Quilting and Quick Quilts Magazines*, *Best Modern Quilts*, *American Quilter Magazine*, *Quilters' Home Magazine*, *Japanese Patchwork Tsushin Magazine*, *Down Under Quilts*, *Irish Quilting Magazine* and *Studios Magazine*. In addition, she has appeared on television and radio programs such as America Quilts Creatively and the American Quilting and Patchwork Radio Show.

With an eye toward making cutting easier for quilters, Kimberly developed a signature line of innovative tools including the EZ Flying Geese Ruler, EZ Jelly Roll Ruler, EZ Hearts Cut Tool, and the EZ Pineapple Ruler for EZ Quilting. She loves to travel and has visited almost every state in America and travelled the world extensively to lecture and teach. She loves to teach quilting on the high seas and has taught on almost two dozen quilting cruises to locales including Alaska, the Caribbean, Mexico and Europe. Most of all, she loves to meet quilters from around the world and share her joy and passion for patchwork and quilting with everyone!

Website: www.kimberlyeinmo.com

Email: Kimberly@kimberlyeinmo.com

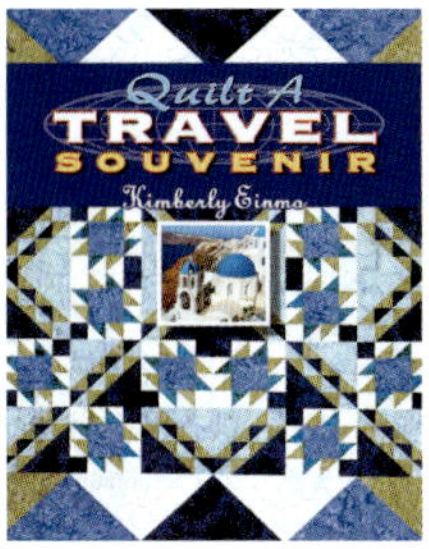

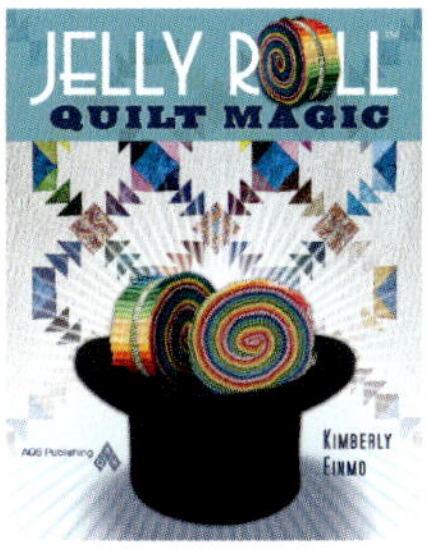